Women, the Arts, and the 1920s in Paris and New York

Women, the Arts, and the 1920s in Paris and New York

Edited by
Kenneth W. Wheeler and Virginia Lee Lussier

Transaction Books
New Brunswick (U.S.A.) and London (U.K.)

Library of Congress Catalog Number: 81-7510
ISBN: 0-87855-908-6
Printed in the United States of America

Library of Congress Cataloging in Publication Data

Main entry under title:

Women, the arts, and the 1920s in Paris and New York.

   Includes bibliographical references and index.
   1. Feminism and the arts—France—Paris—Addresses, essays, lectures.   2. Arts, Modern—20th century—France—Paris—Addresses, essays, lectures.
3. Feminism and the arts—United States—Addresses, essays, lectures.   4. Arts, Modern—20th century—United States—Addresses, essays, lectures.
I. Wheeler, Kenneth W.   II. Lussier, Virginia Lee.
NX180.F4W658   1982   700'.88042   81-7510
ISBN 0-87855-908-6   AACR2

Contents

Acknowledgments

The chapters in this volume were commissioned and presented at the Provost's Conference on Women and the Arts in the 1920s in New York and Paris, held on the New Brunswick campus of Rutgers, the State University of New Jersey on April 6-8, 1978. The three days of conference sessions offered a rich and varied program of papers, exhibits, and performances celebrating creative women in the arts in the 1920s. A luncheon discussion moderated by Richard Poirier included Berenice Abbott, Janet Flanner, Lillian Hellman, and Kay Boyle. Performances included a 1920s cabaret and autobiographic play adaptation of Janet Flanner's *Paris Was Yesterday,* with Celeste Holm playing the role of Ms. Flanner.

Kenneth W. Wheeler, Provost of Rutgers University, New Brunswick campus, recognizing the lack of research on creative women in the 1920s, conceived the conference and guided its overall development. Three years in the planning, the conference was made possible by support from countless individuals and groups. It would be impossible to acknowledge everyone who deserves recognition, but special appreciation is due to the conference planning committee: John Bettenbender, Thomas R. Edwards, Mary S. Hartman, Daniel F. Howard, Julian L. Moynahan, Gloria Orenstein, Jean J. Parrish, Richard Poirier, Elaine C. Showalter, Carol H. Smith, Warren Susman, William A. Walling, and Renée Weber, who met often and worked diligently to give form to the program. Florence Falk, special consultant to the project, provided invaluable professional guidance and direction; Deborah Harper designed and created the exhibits; and Virginia Lee Lussier, assistant provost and academic director of the conference, brought the ideas to functioning reality. Deep appreciation goes to the secretarial staff of the Office of the Provost who gave the conference project their immense energies and dedication.

Financial support for the conference was given by the Associate Alumnae of Douglass College; Joe and Emily Lowe Foundation; National Endowment for the Humanities; New Jersey Committee for the Humanities, an affiliate of the National Endowment for the Humanities; and the Rockefeller Foundation. The National Endowment and the Rockefeller Foundation also provided subvention for the publication of these proceedings.

We are grateful for the guidance, support, and patience of the President and Publisher of Transaction Books, Irving Louis Horowitz and Scott B. Bramson, and to our copy editor Danielle Salti.

Preface

The decade of the 1920s is the most boisterous, bold, imagination-catching period of twentieth-century America. This time of the Roaring Twenties, the Jazz Age, the Era of Wonderful Nonsense, the Boom, the Decade of the Lost Generation, is popularly regarded with bemusement. Serious scholars often seem to have little more insight into its nature than did commentators of the twenties, and many believe that the entire generation whose youth was spent in the twenties must fade away before we can understand the period objectively.

One conclusion is clear: the "flapper" is a prime symbol of the 1920s—and justly so, because movements in America elevated the popular concept of the liberated, autonomous, self-expressive woman to levels unknown before. The record of achievement by American women during this time was mixed, but their role in the arts was often major and at times dominant. On a wall of Harry's New York Bar in Paris is a faded clipping of a photograph puzzle titled "Who Remembers the Twenties: Faces That Made the News in Paris." Of the twenty photographs, twelve featured women. But it is puzzling that women's activities in the twenties have received so little attention by scholars. Studies of women in the United States have focused heavily on periods when major efforts were being made to win political rights for women, such as the mid-nineteenth century, the turn of the twentieth century, and the present. Or they have concentrated on times, such as the

ix

Victorian era, which appeared to be especially repressive for women. We hope the chapters in this volume will stimulate interest in a neglected area.

Various historical factors converged to make the 1920s an extraordinary time for women. The vote had been gained by the Nineteenth Amendment in 1919, and the daughters of the early suffragettes were reaching adulthood. World War I had an immense impact on the generation of the 1920s. Women were affected not only through the men in their families and their lovers, but often by their direct involvement in Europe, as journalists, nurses, or office or factory workers in war production. In 1931, Frederick Lewis Allen described the impact of the war on women:

> American girls . . . had come under the influence of continental manners and standards without being subject to the rigid protections thrown about their continental sisters of the respectable classes; and there had been a very widespread and very natural breakdown of traditional restraints and reticences and taboos. It was impossible for this generation to return unchanged when the ordeal was over. . . . Millions of them had been provided with an emotional stimulant from which it was not easy to taper off. Their town nerves craved the anodynes of speed, excitement, and passion. They found themselves expected to settle down into the humdrum routine of American life as if nothing had happened, to accept the moral dicta of elders who seemed to them still to be living in a Pollyanna land of rosy ideals which the war had killed for them. They couldn't do it, and they very disrespectfully said so.[1]

Another factor which contributed to American women's freedom after the war was the rapid changes in the way people lived at home. Women began to be freed from housework. Millions of Americans moved from houses to apartments; large houses were no longer considered mandatory for the middle class. There was an enormous increase in ready-to-wear apparel, and bakeries, delicatessens, and canned food factories lessened the time required for food preparation. Electric washing machines, electric irons, vacuum cleaners, and refrigerators became standard items in urban middle-class homes. The economy was affluent, jobs were plentiful, and women moved in large numbers into domains previously reserved for men. Women began to play more substantial roles in society. Suffrage was won, the war was won, and women, particularly from middle- and upper-middle-class backgrounds, were expanding their new-won rights. It was a period of new expression, of new cultural and professional independence for women, and an era of redefinition. It was one of the richest decades in Western history for women's achievements.

Most of these activities were rudely brought to a halt by the Great Depression, when millions of women were sent back into their homes by the closing of factories and offices and the decline in expenditures for leisure goods and services. Jobs open to women in the 1920s were turned back to men. Preferential treatment for males, as "family wage earners" was the practice in most employment. Life took on a grim cast in the thirties as the ebullience and creativity of the twenties faded. The public mind of the thirties reacted against "the flapper." The woman of the twenties often came to be regarded in retrospect as vain, flighty, flamboyant, superficial, and even silly. The sensible bobbed hair, cloche hat, short dresses, and reasonable shoes were thought by some to be a lightheaded aberration. By the mid-thirties, a great deal of the aggressive self-expression and independence women had gained in the twenties had been lost and would not return in substantial measure until the late sixties. In some areas such as theater, film, and publishing, women never regained the prominence they held in the 1920s.

Our effort in presenting this volume has been to initiate a reassessment of the role of women in the twenties. We will examine women who were assuming in large numbers influential, key positions in the artistic, literary, and general cultural revolution of the twentieth century. We will appraise their values, the character and interpretation of their work, and their role in society.

The focus on New York and Paris is important. By the 1920s the Chicago renaissance in architecture, art, and literature had faded, and many major participants had moved to New York. Elsewhere in much of the Midwest new elements representing isolationism and reactionary social, cultural, and political values became dominant under Harding's banner of "return to normalcy." New York, now unrivaled as America's literary and artistic capital, had always been exceptional for its tolerance of heterogeneity. It throve on the arrival of intellectuals and artists from America's hinterland. The focus was Greenwich Village and Harlem. Malcolm Cowley in his book *Exiles Return,* written in 1934, tells about the war between *The Saturday Evening Post,* which reflected conservative American middle-class habits and values, and Greenwich Village, which represented those of bohemia, the intellectual and artistic community. As Cowley describes them according to *The Saturday Evening Post:* "The Village was the haunt of affectation . . . inhabited by fools and fakers; . . . the fakers hid Moscow heresies under the disguise of cubism and free verse; . . . the fools would eventually be cured of their folly; they would forget this funny business about art and return to domesticity in South Bend, Indiana." [2] Cowley summarizes the ideas of the Village in the 1920s as self-expression, paganism, living for the moment, liberty, changing place, psychological adjustment, and female equality. Middle America was often threatened by these values, but many of its most talented sons and daughters were mightily attracted by them and came to New York to participate in them.[3] The lure which brought intellectual and artistic Whites to the Village brought their Black counterparts to Harlem, where cultural vitality was so extensive that this era of expression in Black music, dance, theater, and literature came to be known as the Harlem Renaissance.

But New York was not enough for most talented and ambitious intellectuals and artists of the 1920s. Paris had for centuries been a leading world center for intellectual and cultural life, and by 1920 it was still unrivaled. Many left America and New York because of disenchantment with the failures of America's reform efforts, postwar attitudes, the high cost of living, and prohibition mentality. But it was the intellectual and cultural lure of Paris that attracted most. Revolutions in the arts were occurring everywhere; new concepts of architecture, ballet, literature, music, painting, and sculpture flowed into Paris from throughout the world. The City of Light had a special attraction for Americans—the roots of strong Franco-American ties extended to our own Revolutionary era and the end of the nineteenth century saw a major shift from values and tastes that were English and Anglo-Saxon to those of France.[4] For middle- and upper-middle-class creative American women in the arts in the 1920s, it was often the rich and cultivated Edith Wharton, Mary Cassatt, Natalie Barney, and Gertrude Stein who had led the way before World War I. The opening section examines the roles and significance of several pioneers who paved the way for the creative women of the twenties.

NOTES

1. Frederick Lewis Allen, *Only Yesterday: An Informal History of the Nineteen-twenties* (New York: Harper & Bros., 1931), pp. 94-95.
2. Malcolm Cowley, *Exiles Return: A Literary Odyssey of the 1920's* (New York: Viking Press, 1951), p. 53.
3. Ibid.
4. Warren Irving Susman, *Pilgrimage to Paris: The Backgrounds of American Expatriation, 1920-1934* (Ph.D. thesis, University of Wisconsin, 1958).

PART I

Mothers of Us All

Introduction

Catharine R. Stimpson

The Mother of Us All, the title of an opera on which Gertrude Stein and Virgil Thomson once collaborated, may prefigure many of our present concerns. Stein, that massive figure who was both avatar and leader of the avant-garde, finished her libretto in 1946 in Paris, the city in which she was to die a few months later. The composition of *The Mother of Us All* poignantly mingled productivity and its dissolution. The opera was produced in 1947 in New York. The work of two Americans, the culture of expatriates, came home. The mother of us all is the great feminist Susan B. Anthony. Though other figures—Anna Howard Shaw, Daniel Webster, Lillian Russell—appear and reappear, the opera is Anthony's. Her presence reminds us of a fact that both artists and politicians too often evade: the inseparability of power and culture, of politics and the imagination, and of the women's movement and the art that modern women have created.

For many contemporaries, the figure of Stein, like that of Fitzgerald or Hemingway, now evokes a romantic myth about the brilliance and glory of the fun-loving artists in Paris and New York in the 1920s. Tales of their parties, adventures, and aesthetic genius enthrall us, a state in which we may at once believe we have found a nostalgic, secular equivalent of paradise and oversimplify complex realities. Stein also represents the historical importance of the modern city—a New York or Paris—for the modern woman.[1] It was volatile and capricious enough to

3

shelter the daring, innovative, and unpredictable, which the modern woman so often was. If the city was dangerous, it was the arena of the arts, culture, and opportunity. A vital, daring sensibility could flourish in this environment. In Book VII of *The Prelude,* Wordsworth pictures such a setting:

> . . . *the quick dance*
> *Of colours, lights, and forms: the*
>   *deafening din:*
> *The comers and goers face to face,*
> *Face after face; the string of dazzling*
>   *wares.*

The modern city was also dense and populous enough to support collectivities of women, such as the Heterodoxy Club, active in New York in the first part of the twentieth century. Like convents and women's colleges, such groups offered women support for their ambitions, friendship, and relief from a world that might be hostile to both. Finally, the city was financially expansive enough to provide women with ways in which to earn their living. Not everyone in Paris and New York in the 1920s had the small independent income of a Stein, or the large income, which best-sellers augmented, of an Edith Wharton.

If Stein, born in 1874, looked back at Susan B. Anthony, born in 1820, as "a mother," we now look back on Stein and grant her and her generation that status. Yet to think of older, powerful, industrious women as "mothers" may be dangerously misleading. It may permit us to construe the unconventional woman artist conventionally; to conflate her with a maternal role. Ironically, our culture tends to believe that mothers, like Gertrude Morel in *Sons and Lovers,* may inspire their gifted children, but that they are not creative themselves. In brief, "Mothers don't write, they are written." [2]

Biological mothers have been essential to the flesh-and-blood daughters who have gone on to become artists and writers. They have given their girls support, sustenance, and knowledge. Zora Neale Hurston, the Black writer and anthropologist, in her autobiography tenderly remembers the mother who indulged her with stories and fantasies. She tells of a day in Florida, when, looking at a pond, she began to turn landscape into narrative. A visitor warned her not to lie, to talk sense instead, but her mother said to let the child play. Hurston adds reflectively: "Mamma never tried to break me." [3] Yet mother must also be a metaphor, a metonymic trope, an instructive figure that embodies guidance, influence, strength, and experience. Hurston's "mothers" include three other women in New York in the 1920s: Gladys Reichard and Ruth Benedict, who taught her anthropology; and Ethel Waters, whose singing gave her special insights into music.

Such powers entered the lives of women of the 1920s in various ways. Some published children's literature. Their books offered young girls reassuring images of zest, rebellion, and brains. Except for some theoreticians of the avant-garde and some scholarly specialists, we may unfairly stint children's literature. Carolyn Heilburn reminds us of the importance of Louisa May Alcott, who died in 1888, and of her novel *Little Women,* in the formation of the consciousness of modern women. Female writers of children's literature also proved to their readers that women could manipulate style and command the realm of public speech. In her autobiography, Bryher, the English author whose life was entwined with Paris of the 1920s, declares: "We had our problem novelist, Mrs. Molesworth, the Virginia Woolf of the nursery. She wrote on envy, jealousy, and hatred . . . . She . . . understood our fundamental problems . . . . She dominated also because of her style." [4]

Other "mothers" for the women of the 1920s had well-established reputations. Perhaps the most glamorous gift of history to Paris then was Sappho. More than a name, more than an example, more than a handful of fragmented tests, she was an aura to whom statues might be dedicated, an object of reverence merging poetry, outrageous eros, and classical mysteries. Still other women were alive in the 1920s, successful and diligent enough to have a public presence. Chronologically, they stood in relation to younger artists as a parent might to a child. Among them were Edith Wharton, fifty-eight in 1920, spending much of her time in the South of France; Colette, a Frenchwoman, forty-seven in 1920. They were complex, vivid documents about the possibilities of the artist's life.

The women who were beginners in Paris and New York in the 1920s have joined Sappho, Alcott, Colette, Stein, and Cather as "mothers" for those of us who inhabit the 1900s as they end. Like prophecy, influence is neither consistently recognized nor honored. We do not fully know what our mothers may have taught us or wanted us to learn. But they clearly instruct us about the fallibility of the process through which reputations are gained or lost. Though the artist may passionately crave an audience, she should neither expect nor trust it.

As Robert Cottrell warns us in his chapter about Colette, an audience can judge a woman writer on the killing grounds of sex, not talent. Yet women have also found the work of other women, individually and collectively, liberating. The influence of our mothers has been enhancing, not a stimulus for anxiety. It has provoked a sense of release; a belief in women's ability to reject restraint and transgress and transcend the boundaries of ordinary femininity and domesticity.

Our "mothers" teach us that women need not be wives and biological mothers in order to be generative. They demonstrate that some can bear and rear, not children, but a craft. Like a nun, a woman artist can abjure the social and familial obligations of the womb, a choice male artists often fear.[5] Before the 1920s, many women were reasonably convinced that productive work, marriage, and children were incompatible. In *The Mother of Us All* Susan B. Anthony says: "I am not married and the reason why is that I have had to do what I have had to do, I have had to be what I have had to be, I could never be one of two, I could never be two in one." [6] For some, what intimacies they desired could often be happily consummated with other women. As we decipher the history of the 1920s, which our legends have helped obscure, we may conclude that many women of that decade, with great difficulty, attempted to differ from their predecessors and design a fresh integration of work and heterosexual love.

Testing the limits of psychological and artistic freedom, our mothers have helped to free us. Unfortunately, history did not inoculate them against pain, or preserve them entirely from a pact with frailty and struggle. Our mothers were partly sacrificial. As we celebrate them, we must also mourn their trials. They do not beseech our pity, but they might not wholly repudiate a careful recognition of the strains of their modernization. In the final scene of *The Mother of Us All* Gertrude Stein, through Susan B. Anthony, may be asking if we are capable of such a response. Perhaps severely parodying the drama of Don Juan, Stein has Anthony unveiled as a statue. Alone on the stage, the statue's last words speak plainly of wonder, honor, and grief:

> *Life is strife, I was a martyr all my life*
> *   not to what I won but to what was done.*
> *(Silence)*
> *Do you know because I tell you so, or do you know,*
> *   do you know.*
> *(Silence)*
> *My long life, my long life.*[7]

NOTES

1. For some accounts of modern women, see Elaine Showalter (ed.), *These Modern Women: Autobiographical Essays from the Twenties* (Old Westbury, N.Y.: Feminist Press, 1978). Showalter's introduction is exceptionally good.
2. The phrase is from Susan Rubin Suleiman, "Writing and Motherhood," p.

6, paper presented at an MLA Workshop, "The Question of Psychoanalysis in Feminist Criticism," December 1929, San Francisco.
3. Zora Neale Hurston, *Dust Tracks on a Road: An Autobiography* (Philadelphia: J. D. Lippincott, 1942), p. 80.
4. Winifred Bryher, *The Heart to Artemis: A Writer's Memoirs* (New York: Harcourt, Brace, & World, 1962), p. 16. Bryher also notes how important the novels of Dorothy Richardson were to her, in part because she found echoes of her feelings about children's literature in them.
5. To see the persistence of such fears, read a study of the avant-garde in New York in the 1950s and 1960s by Bernard Rosenberg and Norris Fliegel, *The Vanguard Artist: Portrait and Self-Portrait* (Chicago: Quadrangle, 1965).
6. Gertrude Stein, *The Mother of Us All*, in *Last Operas and Plays*, ed. Carl Van Vechten (New York: Rinehart, 1949), p. 75.
7. Stein, p. 88.

1.

Colette's Literary Reputation

Robert D. Cottrell

In 1920, at the age of forty-seven, Sidonie Gabrielle Colette published *Chéri,* the novel that has often been considered quintessential Colette and that firmly established her reputation in France as a popular novelist. With the publication of this novel, Colette's fame, both as a writer and as a "personality," began to equal that of the two other women writers whose literary reputations, although sadly tarnished today, shone brightly in the twenties. Colette soon became as famous as the mercurial Countess Anna de Noailles, whom Janet Flanner in 1933 called "the greatest poetess France has ever possessed," [1] and the prolific novelist Radchilde, who in 1889 had published her first and most notorious novel, *Monsieur Venus,* which prompted the debauch-prone Verlaine to exclaim: "Oh, my dear child! If you could invent a new vice, you would be the benefactress of mankind." [2]

A closer look at the nature of Colette's literary reputation in the twenties (as distinct from her fame as a "personality"—actress, dancer at the Moulin Rouge, journalist, model for the New Woman in the postwar years) reveals that she was invariably praised as a "feminine" writer. In the review of *Chéri* that appeared in 1920 in the *Nouvelle Revue Française,* the most prestigious literary journal of the day, noted critic and novelist Benjamin Cremieux praised Colette's prose as being the best "feminine prose" in French literature.[3] Cremieux declared that

French women writers of earlier generations—Marguerite de Navarre, Madame de Staël, and George Sand among others—"wrote no differently from men," whereas Colette was an exquisite manipulator of "feminine prose."

If French critics of the twenties—male critics, for no woman commented in print on Colette's work until 1928—extolled Colette's literary style, they tended either to ignore or disparage the subject matter of her novels. She was, they all agreed, a supreme stylist, with an infallible sense of rhythms of the French language. Perhaps compelled by a sense of gallantry, they avoided serious consideration of the values implied in her fiction, populated by resilient women and feckless men. Virginia Woolf expressed the problem clearly when she observed late in the twenties that "both in life and in art the values of a woman are not the values of a man." Since the "established values" of society are essentially those of man, the male critic "will see [in a novel written by a woman] not merely a difference of view, but a view that is weak, or trivial, or sentimental, because it differs from his own." [4]

The concept of feminine prose, so often mentioned in the twenties in connection with Colette's work, must be seen in the context of French literature of the first couple of decades of this century. These years were marked by an avalanche of books by dozens of women writers, nearly all of whom have by now sunk below the horizon of critical attention. Readers (or critics) in the twenties saw in Colette's novels not innovation, but an exemplary expression of certain themes that reappeared with obsessive frequency for some twenty years in the mass of books by women authors, themes that help define what was meant in France in the twenties by "feminine" literature.

There appears over and over in those books a particular kind of lyrical celebration of nature. Anna de Noailles, whose rapturous rhetoric is much less appreciated today than it was by an earlier generation, vibrated tinglingly as she felt herself in tune with all of nature. "I was star, foliage, wing, scent, cloud." [5] Although Colette eschewed Anna de Noailles' grandiloquence and ornateness, in the twenties her fame rested in part, as it does today, on her ability to evoke flowers, plants, and the various moods of nature with a lucidity, tough-mindedness, and tender anthropomorphism unique in French literature. For Colette, as for most women writers of the time, nature was a garden, an enclosure that approximated a room of her own. It was a refuge from the murky world of society, often Parisian society, from the hypocrisy of men.

If nature figures prominently in the feminine literature of the first twenty years of this century, so does the human body. Reacting against the nineteenth-century tendency to study "sentiment" as if it were an entity isolated from the body, French women writers at the beginning of our century sang caressingly and sensuously of their bodies, which they perceived as being in communion with nature. There is a reflection of this fusion of the female body and nature in the *art nouveau* of the period, for here too the flowing lines of the hair and limbs often merge with plants to become part of the general configuration of voluptuous, curvilinear forms.

A character in Colette's fiction, who more than likely possesses no mind to speak of, is above all a corporeal presence. Her female characters are often shown peering into a mirror, scrutinizing their face, neck, shoulders, and arms for signs of fatigue or aging. They examine each others' bodies lucidly and harshly, as if they were examining fruit or vegetables at the market. With even greater care, they examine the male body, or rather the body of a male adolescent with long eyelashes, graceful limbs, and just barely defined pectorals. In *The Last of Chéri* two aging cocottes discuss the strong and weak points of a man they both know:

> "Oh, my dear, what a disappointment! Tall, yes, that goes without saying . . . in point of fact, rather too tall. I'm still waiting to be shown one, just one who is well put together. Eyes, yes, eyes, I've got nothing to say against his eyes. But—from here to there, don't you see (she was pointing to her own face), from here to there, something about the cheeks which is too rounded, too soft, and the ears set too low . . . oh, a very great disappointment. And holding himself as stiff as a poker."
>
> "You're exaggerating," said Lea. "The cheeks—well what about cheeks? they aren't so very important. And, from here to there, well really it's beautiful, it's noble; the eyelashes, the bridge of the nose, the eyes, the whole thing is really too beautiful! I'll grant you the chin: that will quickly run to flesh. And the feet are too small, which is ridiculous in a boy of that height."
>
> "No, there I don't agree with you. But I certainly noticed that the thigh was far too long in proportion to the leg, from here to there."
>
> They went on to thrash out the question, weighing up, with a wealth of detail and point by point, every portion of the fore and hind quarters of this expensive animal.[6]

An unsettling scene bordering on the indecent? Probably, at least from a male reader's point of view, but couched, as is always the case in Colette, in language of the kind she found in *Lady Chatterly's Lover*. In 1932 she wrote to Lady Troubridge, who had sent her a copy of D.H. Lawrence's novel: "What do you think of this poor childish excited

person, the author of Lady-What's-Her Name's Lover? It's terribly adolescent and immature. . . . What a narrow province obscenity is, suf-
focating and boring." [7] Colette's own fiction depicts a milieu of loose
morals, seductive and unscrupulous courtesans, aging roués, baby-faced
gigolos, painted denizens of Sodom and Gomorrah. Yet her characters,
at least her female protagonists, have an inflexible sense of propriety
and morality, which has little to do with an official code of morals.

Many French women writers of the first two decades of this century,
evoking their bodies in a kind of pantheistic rapture, found men intol-
erably crude, insensitive, pretentious. Hence another feature of this
literature: an astonishing proliferation of books that deal, discreetly and
lyrically, with lesbianism or, to use the word preferred by the writers
themselves, sapphism. As portrayed in this literature, lesbianism is the
impulse of a tender, often bruised feminine spirit that finds comfort by
seeing itself reflected in a kindred spirit. Emerging from their whalebone corsets and multiple petticoats like a butterfly from its chrysalis,
French women writers often introduced sapphism in their work as a
means of expressing a sensuality no longer brutalized, lacerated, or
denied. This sapphic melody, bittersweet and verging on the elegiac, is a
narcissistic celebration of self. Sapphism in this literature is, like nature,
a refuge, an asylum, a sanctuary. Criticizing Proust for having misrepre-
sented lesbianism in *Remembrance of Things Past,* Colette wrote that
"two women enlaced will never be for a man anything but a depraved
couple, and not the melancholic and touching image of two weak beings
who have perhaps taken refuge in each other's arms, there to sleep and
weep, to flee from man who is often cruel, and to taste, better than any
pleasure, the bitter happiness of feeling that they are alike, small,
forgotten." [8]

This view of lesbianism may seem quaint and outmoded today, too
bittersweet to be in fashion. Colette's depiction of sapphism is representative of the way it was treated by French women writers in the early
years of this century. Celebration of nature, preoccupation with the
body, and interest in lesbianism are subsumed in the larger and more
general theme of love. Perhaps at no period in French literature has
love been analyzed more deftly, more variously than in the books
published by the now forgotten women writers of the first two decades
of the twentieth century. Of these authors, many of whom offered subtle
insights into the nature of love, only Colette is read today.

On those rare occasions when critics in the twenties alluded to the
values expressed in Colette's fiction, in Colette's view they were hostile.
The remarks of Colette's second husband, the aristocratic Henri de

Jouvenel, newspaper editor and politician, are typical. She reports that he said to her: "Can't you write a book that is not about love or adultery or a semi-incestuous relationship or a parting? Isn't there anything else in life?" [9] Jean-Paul Sartre, writing much later but in the same vein, observed that "a woman's book is one that refuses to take into account what men do. Many men have never written anything but feminine books." [10] Sartre was not speaking specifically about Colette when he made this comment, but Simone de Beauvoir was when she said disapprovingly that Colette "was after all very much engrossed in little stories about love, housekeeping, and animals." [11]

These remarks by Sartre and Simone de Beauvoir suggest why Colette exerted so little influence on the writers who emerged as the dominant and most powerful figures of the thirties and forties in France. Like most women writers of her generation, she did not "take into account what men were doing." In the fifties, novelist and journalist Claudine Chonez commented bitterly that women writers of Colette's generation "missed out on surrealism, missed out on the broad movement toward the social novel before 1914, missed out on the postwar anxieties." [12] Many male writers did too. But the generation of writers born in the first years of this century, who in the twenties were writing or publishing their first books, were determined not to miss out. Most of these younger writers, such as Simone de Beauvoir and Simone Weil, had not only been university-trained but trained specifically in philosophy. Literature to them meant something very different from what it meant to Colette, whose formal education had ceased at the equivalent of junior high school. Political events in Europe during the thirties, especially the Spanish Civil War and the ever-increasing threat of World War II, made Colette's work, with its faint fin-de siècle aroma, almost as remote as the century of Louis XVI.

During the thirties and forties Colette continued to write, producing the serene, majestic, and exquisitely mannered books of her old age, on which her reputation may ultimately rest. That her voice remained perfectly pitched was, all the younger writers agreed, astonishing. But she was thought of as being outside the mainstream. When Germaine Bree and Margaret Guiton published their influential *An Age of Fiction: The French Novel from Gide to Camus* in 1957, they did not discuss Colette. In their preface they observed that Colette "remained aloof from the principal currents of the time." After her death in 1954, Colette was not forgotten in France, but her books were set aside. So were they in this country. In the early thirties, an American reader could have bought an English translation of most of Colette's novels. In

1973, only four were in print in the United States. Since then, almost all her novels have been reissued in this country.

NOTES

1. Janet Flanner, *Paris Was Yesterday, 1925–1939,* ed. Irving Drutman (New York: Viking, 1972), p. 93.
2. Quoted by André David, *Radchilde* (Paris: Editions La Nouvelle Revue Critique, 1924), p. 22. Unless indicated otherwise, all translations in this article are my own.
3. Benjamin Cremieux, *La Nouvelle Revue Française* 15 (1920): 938–40.
4. Virginia Woolf, *Granite and Rainbow: Essays* (New York: Harcourt, Brace, 1958), p. 81.
5. Quoted by Evelyn Sullerot, *Histoire et mythologie de l'amour: huit siècles d'écrits féminins* (Paris: Hachette, 1974), p. 230. This is probably the best survey of French women writers from the Middle Ages to the present.
6. Sidonie Gabrielle Colette, *Chéri* and *The Last of Chéri,* trans. Roger Senhouse (New York: Farrar, Straus, & Young, 1951), p. 218. In the past few years, several critical works have been published that study the significance of the body in Colette's fiction: Marcelle Biolley-Godino, *L'Homme objet chez Colette* (Paris: Klincksieck, 1972); Elaine Harris, *L'Approfondissement de la sensualité dans l'oeuvre romanesque de Colette* (Paris: Nizet, 1973); Yannich Rech, *Corps féminin, corps sensuel: essais sur le personnage féminin dans l'oeuvre de Colette* (Paris: Klincksieck, 1973).
7. Quoted by Yvonne Mitchell, *Colette: Taste for Life* (London: Weidenfeld & Nicolson, 1975), p. 91.
8. Sidonie Gabrielle Colette, *La Vagabonde,* vol. 4 of the Fleuron edition of *Oeuvres complètes* (1948–50), p. 191. In the English-language translation, *The Vagabond* (New York: Farrar, Straus, & Young, 1955), this passage is on p. 188.
9. Sidonie Gabrielle Colette, *La Naissance du jour,* vol. 8 of the Fleuron edition, pp. 18–19. In the English-language translation, *Break of Day* (New York: Farrar, Straus, & Cudahy, 1960), this passage is on pp. 18–19.
10. Jean-Paul Sartre, *Situations IX* (Paris: Gallimard, 1972), pp. 18–19.
11. Quoted by Biolley-Godino, *L'Homme objet,* p. 140.
12. Claudine Chonez, "Hier, aujourd'hui, demain," *La Table Ronde* 99 (March 1956): 63.

2.

Willa Cather: A Problematic Ideal

Ann Douglas

Willa Cather is perhaps the most influential woman writer of this century. Her influence on other women writers such as Carson Mc-Cullers, Katherine Anne Porter, Eudora Welty, is well known. I have chosen to write about her, less for her direct influence than for her quality as an exemplary figure among women writers. I will not confine my remarks to the 1920s, but address myself to her career and corpus as a whole. Willa Cather may be an ideal figure for women writers and, for that very reason, suspect. She achieved a scope and serenity which, while enviable and representative of goals for all women writers who have followed her, have also seemed to exclude certain aspects of the female experience that have triggered some of our most important feminine writing.

When I first saw a picture of Willa Cather a number of years ago, I was taken aback. It was a frontispiece to a book entitled *Willa Cather: A Memoir,* by Elizabeth Sargeant. Willa Cather is standing facing the camera forthrightly; her eyes meet yours. She is holding a walking stick in both hands. She is palpably honest and self-possessed. Acclimatized, like most women, to small social lies, even to the dodgings of larger self-deceptions, I do not expect or trust integrity in my own sex. After all, lying suggests that one has not given in. Tacit and communal deceit is a recognized badge of oppression. I closed Sargeant's book with an odd

14

sense of discomfort. One thing was clear: I could not call Cather my own as I claimed both lesser and greater women writers. That was the indisputable point of her disquieting photograph which pictured a face far more alien to me than George Eliot's or Sylvia Plath's. It was not simply her colossal indifference to the crisis of her own society. "Industrial life has to work out its own problems," she once remarked as she dismissed the contemporary world. It was her invulnerability, her almost biological ability not to pay the price of which her lack of social conscience was but a symptom that distanced and troubled me. Early biographers of Cather who knew her, friends like Elizabeth Sargeant and Edith Lewis, hint at depressions, moods of anger, sexual ambiguities, fits of loneliness, and one wonders what was in all those letters she ordered destroyed. The fact remains that Cather did not sleep with monsters, as Adrienne Rich has said a thinking woman must do. Cather was liberated from certain torture chambers which have confined her equally talented sisters.

This is not to assert that only women writers have been neurotics or outsiders, but rather to suggest that neurosis and alienation have constituted peculiarly their portion, even their identity. Yet Cather did not write, chart, or analyze intensities of anxiety and pain. Her power came from her incipient complacency, checked only by her omnipresent sense of the fragility of history. What right did she have, a woman in this society, not to suffer? What can she offer us now? In novels like *A Lost Lady* (1923) and *My Mortal Enemy* (1926), Cather described with penetration complex and neurotic relationships between men and women, yet love was not her subject. *A Lost Lady* is less a neurotic woman entangled in affairs, though she is that, than an emblem of a fading vision of a special social order in the South. Cather's culture did not have that power over her it wields over many of its gifted women forced to register and respond to experiences for whose existence and dimensions they have only partial responsibility. Cather's artistic role is never that of the allowed, if outraged, interloper. Cather makes no perilous forays from a precarious and threatened retreat. She is no spy in enemy territory. Cather loses in a certain type of sensitivity what she gains in strength. Although she often writes about women, she is not leashed to the feminine consciousness as so many of even the best women authors have admitted or shown themselves to be. Her central characters in her later books are male. They are Roman Catholic prelates, men of devotion in *Death Comes for the Archbishop* and *Shadows on the Rock*, men dedicated to the service of the Virgin, but men nonetheless. Humanity itself is Cather's theme. She has a calmness of scope. She writes as a woman only in the sense that Tolstoy wrote as a man. What other major woman aside from Emily Brontë has such a sense of space? She does not seem to need a room of her own: she has a world.

In the ranks of women authors Cather has a special place. George Eliot, Harriet Beecher Stowe, even Virginia Woolf or Sylvia Plath, so different and terrible in their proximity to fragmentation, suffering, and self-destruction, claim nothing but their consciousness even while their claims for it were great. All were willing to renounce the perilous struggle to possess for the intangible power to haunt. Theirs was the cult of the posthumous heroine: Little Eva, wafting inexorably toward heavenly regions; Dorothea Brook and Maggie Tuliver, with their anchorite if myopic insistence of self-denial; Mrs. Dalloway barely recovered from heart disease, disembodied, nearly invisible if inescapable; Plath, who earned the privilege of prophecy in antique mad Cassandra style. Cather's heroines tend to be survivors. They turn up like Mrs. Forester of *A Lost Lady* in the new countries with new and questionable men. They may, like Antonia of *My Antonia,* frankly reveal the ravages of time. But they usually prefer to laugh, to live. Cather had a zest for ownership, foreign to her feminine predecessors and successors. She urges her readers not to exhaust their territory but to redefine it and their claims to it. She does not hover, she does not dissolve and disarm her perceptions as Woolf did. She does not need the dynamic energy which propelled Plath and Stowe to salute their destroyers. She does not choose with Eliot to use self-mutilation as protest.

Cather has no substitutes for rebellion. She bypasses it altogether. "Mine," she says calmly, carving out in those short, simple, breathtakingly right sentences her own detailed, crystalline, and transfigured territory. In the twenties, the great movement among authors male and female was often toward expatriation. Sarah Orne Jewett, a predecessor of Cather and probably the writer whom Cather felt she owed the most to, ended her best work—*The Country of the Pointed Firs,* written in 1896—with a picture of her narrator being rapidly borne away from Bennett's Landing, Maine, that decaying coastal town which embodies the finest of the American past. Later come the novels and poems of actual expatriation, proliferating denials of the American continent. Cather will have none of this. Her moment of transfiguration is one of discovery or recovery. Her novels regress back over time to return to the settler experience; the frail but actual moment of catching hold. Cather is after the cure, the help of possession. "Art should simplify," she once wrote. As a woman and artist, she lived out the fight of reduction, the compression necessary for great yield, in an intense effort to find out what was her own and no one else's.

Cather was born in Nebraska and moved fairly rapidly toward New York. She worked as a muckraker for a while on *McClure's Magazine* in New York, but left journalism by 1912 and never went back to it. She had early decided never to marry. "Married nightingales do not sing," she believed. Whether this choice was dictated by the needs of her own temperament or by some abstract artistic considerations, it was the right one for her. She had many intense friendships with women. She had enormous respect for her own creative strengths and weaknesses. She made the theme of her life a recessional of dignity and decision. The simplicity for which she strove was that ritual simplification by which debts are paid and questions of ownership resolved. Cather presents her fictive world as if it were one, *the one* we have always known. Her instinct for possession is so sure that it functions as a ritual of recovery. Nothing establishes Cather's role as heir better than her refusal to litigate, her reliance on simple testimony of recognition. She disliked to introduce her characters formally to her readers. In *My Antonia* one of Antonia's friends, Lena Lingard, entering the kitchen when Antonia is working in Black Hawk, is presented just as she appears to Antonia, who knows her well. Only gradually do we learn her background, in the same natural offhand way we might make an acquaintance. The Archbishop in *Death Comes for the Archbishop* makes his debut as a man riding across the landscape. Cather will not dislodge her characters from their surroundings to satisfy her readers' curiosity. Respect for their positioning is the first and supreme law of her art. Her sense of wholeness and integrity is so strong that it dictates her perspectives and her story. She never allows her readers to grasp her stories in any usual sense. She calmly withholds and diffuses climaxes, insistent that her characters' lives are communally defined, not dramas sparked by individual and psychological motives. She will not violate history.

Cather's perspective is always distant: Antonia viewed and created in terms of accumulated time; the Archbishop seen birdseye amid the desert; the "Lost Lady" remembered by those who had loved her. The Jamesian technique of microscopic inspection and dissection was finally not for Cather. It smacked fatally of a kind of disbelief. Her art, in her greatest works, was increasingly one of benediction. Very materially, in *My Antonia*, for Antonia has that most conventional gift of God, a full womb; she has numerous offspring, who pour forth at one highly symbolic moment from the cellar to greet the returned narrator of the novel. More spiritually, in *Death Comes for the Archbishop* and *Shadows on the Rock*, for the ecclesiastical heroes they find a final blessing in self-sacrifice.

Cather's subject is America itself. Her question is "who owns America?" Cather began her career as a populist manqué. She ended it as a firm aristocrat. Yet she never lost her conviction that America belongs not to the industrialists who exploit its resources, not to the politicians who manipulate its inhabitants, not to the intellectuals who analyze its significance, but to the men and perhaps even more the women who work and cherish its land. Antonia, and Alexander Bergson in *O Pioneers!* are in possession, while the cultivated semiprofessional men who love them, Jim Burden and Carl Linstrom, are expatriates in their own country. The characters for whom Cather cares most deeply are preoccupied with the religious dignity of labor, duty, the art of turning time into tradition. Theirs are the domestic tasks of getting territory and preserving customs, the processes of civilization itself. They build and keep houses, till the land, missionize the wilderness, venerate their ancestors. At their finest, characters like Professor St. Peter in *The Professor's House,* the Archbishop in *Death Comes for the Archbishop,* or Cécile in *Shadows on the Rock* share Cather's belief in the corrective bite of the sparseness of history. Cécile, looking after her father with scrupulous care, almost a child herself, is at first upholding her dead mother's standards of bourgeois French housekeeping in newly settled and primitive seventeenth-century Quebec. Later she finds that this is not routine but a ritual whose significance goes deeper than duty, deeper even than identity, past the self into ecclesia. In Cécile's discipline is her title deed. She is to stay in the New World and bring forth sons to populate it. Unlike so many literary heroines, she has found her place, not just in men's minds, not just in literature, but on the land and its history. Nothing marks more surely Cather's confidence than the historic cast of her best narratives.

Here I take leave of Willa Cather unquestionably in possession of a totally imaginative and rich world. She established her claims to the past she believed contained almost all that was valuable in the present, to the continent which embodied and betrayed the premises of faith. She had respect for history, precision of priorities, shared management of limited resources. She had that frugality which finds the precious meat at retrenchment's marrow. Her message is for the dispossessed, perhaps for women chief among them. Yet she bears no scars, the customary stripes of sisterhood. She is intact. Ambition has a lofty place in Cather's world. Thea Kronberg in a *Song of the Lark* struggles as cleanly to escape the provinces as Cather herself did. The only thing Cather failed to realize was the meaning of the oppression. The price she paid was the incalculable cost of a determined serenity. Cather offers us an ideal; she offers us a remedy. But we can and must complain that she has not herself fully experienced, explored, and documented the disease.

SELECTED BIBLIOGRAPHY

Edward Killoran Brown, *Willa Cather: A Critical Biography* (New York: Knopf, 1953).

David Daiches, *Willa Cather: A Critical Introduction* (Ithaca: Cornell University Press, 1951).

James Leslie Woodress, *Willa Cather: Her Life and Art* (New York: Pegasus, 1970).

Lucia Woods, *Willa Cather: A Pictorial Memoir* (Lincoln: University of Nebraska Press, 1973).

3.

Louisa May Alcott:
The Influence of *Little Women*

Carolyn G. Heilbrun

The influence of *Little Women* upon women artists in Paris between the wars is a matter of faith. As the Bible tells us, faith is the evidence of things not seen. If only Gertrude Stein had written of Jo March, or at least stopped into Sylvia Beach's bookshop and requested *Little Women.* What she requested, I am constrained by truth to report, is *The Trail of the Lonesome Pine* and *A Girl of the Limberlost.*[1] There is a reference to Alcott in Stein's writing, but not to *Little Women.* It is to *Rose in Bloom,* and Stein is reminded of it by the New Englanders' fear of drinking: "I always remembered it in *Rose in Bloom* and how they worried about offering any one a drink and even about communion wine, any one in that way might suddenly find they had a taste for wine."[2]

Sylvia Beach mentions *Little Women* only as the source of a joke on Frank Harris who, rushing to make a train, was in search of something "exciting" to read. Beach asked him if he had read *Little Women* which, rendered into French as *Petites femmes,* connoted something exciting to a man of Harris' tastes. He was resentful of being locked in a train for hours with such an appalling lack of eroticism.[3] Thornton Wilder, who knew Stein and many of the others, evokes *Little Women* in *The Eighth Day,* supposedly not for the first time. But is any of this evidence?

Yet I do not admit that my faith in *Little Women* as an influence consists solely of the substance of things hoped for. Everyone read *Little*

Women—there is evidence enough for that; certainly every prepubescent female absorbed that book with the air she breathed. My own children—just to show you the extent and persistence of the influence—went to school with four sisters named Meg, Jo, Amy, and Beth. Unfortunately, no one could notice that Jo differed perceptibly from the others. But in the book itself, Jo differed more than perceptibly: Jo was a miracle. She may have been the single female model continuously available after 1868 to girls dreaming beyond the confines of a constricted family destiny to the possibility of autonomy and experience initiated by one's self.

We literary critics welcome complexities which challenge our carefully honed talents and enable us to unravel novels whose profundities can be suspected of escaping the untrained reader. Complex novels and poems are meat and drink to critics, but children are more in the position of the puzzled ice cream manufacturer who asked Wallace Stevens if in "The Emperor of Ice Cream" he was for ice cream or against it. We forget sometimes, though Frank Kermode has reminded us, that "fictions are for finding things out." [4] One of the things they are for finding out is the process of growing from a girl into a woman. Men may ask pretty girls: "Are there any more at home like you?" Most girls may, in the past, have considered that a pretty question. But girls who were going to grow up and go to Paris were more likely to have exclaimed with Jo: "I hate affected, niminy-piminy chits. I hate to think I've got to grow up, and be Miss March, and wear long gowns and look as prim as a China-aster. . . . I can't get over my disappointment in not being a boy." Beth soothes Jo by assuring her she can be a brother to them all, and Jo, to be sure, in her father's absence, recognizes herself as "the man of the family."

Jo's is an identification only possible in those innocent days when one could say what one felt without being accused of nameless, or worse, named Freudian perversions. Jo recognized (along with her readers) that girls such as she, few enough in number, *were* ideally the fathers of their families because there was no other model. Such girls might want to care for their mothers; they certainly did not wish to imitate them. Who in her right mind (which few girls were in those dark days) would want to imitate such a creature? Marmee's vision of a woman's role in marriage is enough to turn the stomach, and the exceptional young reader could declare with Jo: "I wasn't meant for a life like this."

Great books are so identified because they turn out, a century or so later, to have been amazingly prescient. Today, armed with the data and insights of all those social sciences focusing their attention upon achieving women, we recognize that Alcott provided for Jo those conditions likeliest to produce this interesting creature. While Alcott depended upon the facts of her own life, she nonetheless transmuted them into a pattern of female selfhood. Reviewers might attribute the success of *Little Women* to the threefold accomplishment of preserving the family as the foundation of the republic, making female adolescence into a life stage, and picturing loving self-sacrifice according to female dreams [5]—but beyond all this is Alcott's recognition of the opportunity her all-girl family had provided for her own development.

Bronson Alcott, at the birth of his fourth female child, noted that her birth manifested God's will that the Alcotts be content to "rear women for the future world." [6] Whatever God's will, if any, in the matter, girls without brothers are far likelier to end up as true women of the future world, questioning the conventional female destiny. Achieving women are statistically likely to be from all-girl families. Margaret Hennig, for example, examining top-range women managers in business firms, of whom there were not many, discovered that all the women in her sample were only children or from all-girl families—an extraordinary statistical finding. These girls were brotherless and therefore qualified as "sons." Louisa and her older sister were objects of educational experiments by their father: he had no sons on whom to apply them. Not uncommonly, if the unconventional woman is not the only or oldest child, she will be the one among a father's daughters selected by him as his "son." Writer Dorothy Richardson, for example, was "odd girl out" for her father: third among his four daughters, the child with whom he formed a union against a household of "women." [7] Louisa, we know, was Bronson Alcott's "son." [8]

While the tomboy character has long been a staple of life and fiction, most tomboys exist in relation to boys; certainly those of fiction do so, emulating and envying their brothers. These tomboys may be teased as hoydens, but they are not recognized as sons, as the independent ones among weaker women. Maggie Tulliver, for example, in George Eliot's *The Mill on the Floss,* creates herself in emulation and adoration of her brother Tom. Their father may mourn that it is the wench who is the smart one, but it is Tom who will get the education. For Jo, male destiny may be envied, but not in the person of a brother. Similarly, in an all-girl school girls may win the attention of teachers and aspire to positions not automatically considered the property of males: there are no males. Laurie in this eccentric book is made to look with envy on the happy female world.

A word of caution is necessary regarding girls chosen by their fathers as "sons." He does not think of her nor does the girl think of herself as a boy. Penis envy, despite Freud's strictures rigidified with the eager help of his female followers, is not the issue. These young women never doubt their core gender identity. They inhabit female bodies gladly, and dream, not of male anatomy, but of male autonomy. Here Alcott was again both naive and, in the wonderful freedom of that naiveté, prescient. She knew that for women who considered Marmee's destiny, or Meg's, impossible for themselves, the only model was a male model— she adopted it.

Women have been trapped here. The world, wishing to keep them in their place, where the world found it very convenient for them to be, warned them that if they did not accept the female role they would lose their femininity and become, moreover, monsters: imitation men. It followed that in imitating men they were also robbing them of their masculinity. This has to be the most extraordinary double bind in history. Jo could be so clear about her choice between male and female destinies, at least for half the book, because no one had arrived to tell her that she was courting some hideous Freudian disaster. The chosen "son" within the all-girl family, Jo was free to follow the male model, the only acceptable one around.

Jo plays the male parts in plays, wears a "gentlemanly" collar and has a gentlemanly manner, thinks of herself as a businessman and cherishes a pet rat. (The pet rat is male and has a son, "proud of his whiskers," who accompanies him along the rafters.) Jo finds it easier to risk her life for a person than to be pleasant when she does not want to, and she admires the "manly" way of shaking hands. The point is clear: men's manners speak of freedom, openness, comradery, physical abandon, the chance to escape passivity. Who would not prefer such a destiny, except those taught to be afraid?

Strictures against women imitating the male model are universal. Even today if one recommends the male model for women (shorn of its machismo and denigration of women), one is likely to startle everyone. But Jo knew that there was no other, and that to search for female models makes good history but poor consolation. Jo knew that in a conventional family pattern, where the mother could recommend only her own confinement, there was no other model than the father. Some women indeed provided another model. Where did they discover it? Partly, in a young fictional creature who, as Natalie Barney was to say of Gertrude Stein, "had such faith in herself as passeth understanding." [9]

In the end, Alcott betrayed Jo. Women have great difficulty imagining autonomous females (even if they have managed to become one) and sustaining the imaginative creation once they have achieved it. Jo had to be more or less conventionally "disposed of." [10] Those who hold to the romantic view of tomboys resent the fact that Jo had to marry a German twice her age. Alcott could not, apparently, prevent Jo's marrying, but she could and did prevent her marrying Laurie, despite the demands of her publisher and public. When Jo's father returns from the war to this female world, he "compliments" Jo by saying that he does not see the "son, Jo" whom he left a year hence. "I see a young lady who . . ." and there follows an account of a young lady's attributes. We feel sold. Alcott will tell us at the end of *Little Women* that spinsters "have missed the sweetest part of life" (how persistently women buy that line!) despite the fact that she signed her letters from Europe in the months following the success of *Little Women* "spinsterhood forever," and when asked for advice to give girls, told them of "the sweet independence of the spinster's life." [11] Alcott was confused in her fictional, if not in her usual mind, but her biographers muddle the two. The latest, Martha Saxton, writes as though not finding a man to marry were a failure explicable only by psychological wounds.

Of course, Jo starts a school for boys. Who would want to mess around with silly girls? If you cannot change the destiny of girls, you can at least take on the education of the sex with some chance of freedom and accomplishment outside of domesticity. The feeling is most commonly reflected in the woman's wish for male children, as Adrienne Rich tells us: "When I first became pregnant I set my heart on a son. (In our childish, acting-out games I had always preferred the masculine roles and persuaded or forced my younger sister to act the feminine ones.) I still identified more with men than with women; the men I knew seemed less held back by self-doubt and ambivalence, more choices seemed open to them. I wanted to give birth, at twenty-five, to my unborn self—someone independent, actively willing, original." [12]

Once one has opted to support the male system and put one's ambitions, as Jo does, into the raising of boys, one writes of Meg's twins as though stereotyped destinies for the sexes were among the eternal verities. There may be something more sickening than little Daisy, but where to find it outside the precepts of the Total Woman movement, I do not know. It has been argued, most persuasively by Nina Auerbach in her excellent study of female communities, that in the end Jo becomes "a cosmic mother," the greatest power available in that domestic world.[13] Jo was the girl who embodied the impossible girlhood dreams, and not the young female who became—heaven forbid—a mother.

Jo's readers probably overlooked the conventional ending. Jo wanted to end up, when she knew she could not become free as a man, as a "literary spinster," an apt way to describe the women in Paris between the wars. Jo's youthful experiences may have provided a model for sisterhood, as Nina Auerbach so well demonstrates. The all-girl family in Austen's *Pride and Prejudice*, Auerbach points out, lives in an empty world, awaiting rescue by men.[14] The March world is complete in itself; there women suffice to each other for happiness, and "permanent sisterhood is a felt dream rather than a concrete possibility."[15] Auerbach further suggests that in giving the family the name of a month, Alcott took her mother, whose maiden name was May, as the true progenitor of the family, the source of energy and possibility. To me Alcott's portrayal of sisterhood is too sentimental, too doomed by marital conventions both as to its present and future; yet it is, for all that, a memorable dream of sisterhood, perhaps the one fictional world where young women, complete unto themselves, are watched with envy by a lonely boy.

Alcott's other literary works, with Jo or without her, are certainly of interest, especially *Work*, yet they appeal perhaps more to the feminist historian and critic than to the girl reader. We recognize with pleasure that in *An Old Fashioned Girl* there is a community of women artists, and that in an unpublished fragment of an adult novel Alcott, most enticingly, has a woman say: "Do not look for meaning in marriage, that is too costly an experiment for us. Flee from temptation and do not dream of spoiling your life by any commonplace romance."[16] But these fragments, these interpretations, are what the critics find. For youngsters, reading in search of legends they need not even consciously acknowledge or remember, it is Jo who is immortal.

What must be emphasized is her uniqueness. She is a myth, alone and unchallenged—peerless. For she has the whole business absolutely straight as a child, an adolescent. Maybe Alcott did not know what to do with her when she grew up, but Barney, Stein, and Flanner knew what to do with themselves when they grew up, and I am inclined to give Jo part of the credit. Perhaps remembered only dimly, children's literature, safe as homes, she nonetheless expressed, as few had, what it felt like to be a girl who was not going to grow up conventionally female and knew it when she was very young. Because there was no fantasy in Jo's end, her beginnings were believable. Romance promised a prince. *Little Women* promised whatever you could make of your life; anyway, not the boy next door. What Stein, Barney, Toklas, and Beach made of their lives, we know or will learn here. I want to suggest Jo as the daimon, the unique girl who dared to speak as they felt. Alcott, who created her, was not the mother of us all, but Jo was, and not because she became a cosmic mother in fiction. In fiction her children were boys. In life, her true children were girls who grew up and went to Paris and did wonderful things.

NOTES

1. Sylvia Beach, *Shakespeare and Company* (New York: Harcourt, Brace, 1959), p. 28.
2. Gertrude Stein, *Everybody's Autobiography* (New York: Random House, 1937), p. 237.
3. Beach, *Shakespeare,* p. 92.
4. Frank Kermode, *The Sense of an Ending* (New York: Oxford University Press, 1967), p. 39.
5. Sarah Elbert, Introduction to *Work* by Louisa May Alcott (New York: Schocken Books, 1977), p. xviii.
6. Ibid., p. xi.
7. Horace Gregory, *Dorothy Richardson: An Adventure in Discovery* (New York: Holt, Rinehart, & Winston, 1967), p. 19.
8. Martha Saxton, *Louisa May Alcott* (Boston: Houghton Mifflin, 1977), p. 256.
9. Linda Simon (ed.), *Gertrude Stein: A Composite Portrait* (New York: Discus Books, 1974), p. 44.
10. Patricia Spacks, *The Female Imagination* (New York: Knopf, 1975), p. 100.
11. Mary Jane Moffat and Charlotte Painter (eds.), *Revelations: Diaries of Women* (New York: Random House, 1974), p. 29.
12. Adrienne Rich, *Of Women Born* (New York: Norton, 1976), p. 193.
13. Nina Auerbach, "Austen and Alcott on Matriarchy," Radcliffe Institute Reprint, p. 24. See Nina Auerbach, *Communities of Women: An Idea in Fiction* (Cambridge, Mass.: Harvard University Press, 1978).
14. Idem, "Austen and Alcott," p. 17.
15. Ibid., p. 24.
16. Quoted in ibid., p. 23.

4.

Gertrude Stein: The Complex Force of Her Femininity

Cynthia Secor

Gertrude Stein is not primarily a writer of the 1920s, although she is commonly discussed in that context. She wrote from 1903 to 1946, steadily gaining in mastery and continuing to experiment with the language. As Carl Van Vechten has said, she influenced three generations of writers—as Spenser and Milton influenced subsequent generations. Any serious writer coming after her had to take into account her use of language, for to write in English without paying attention to her exploration of the possibilities of the language would be delinquent. Her influence covers a range of writers as diverse as Cocteau, Cummings, Van Vechten, Hemingway, Wilder, Anderson, Sutherland, O'Hara, Wright, Beckett, and Ionesco. Realist, absurdist, classicist, can all be shown to bear her mark.

Yet there is lack of understanding by these same writers, their contemporaries, and the critical establishment regarding her work. She is of the "inaccessible" generation of Joyce, Eliot, and Pound, yet she alone has been singled out as inaccessible. Her contemporaries at once responded to her warmly and commented on her giant ego or childlike complacency. The latter comments often come from those jealous of her reputation, which grew steadily over forty years of writing, unsustained by such conventional props as critical success, publication, and a wide reading public.

How then to explain Stein's continuing impact on serious writers over the seventy-five years since she began writing? How to explain the steadiness and confidence with which she continued her work despite the upheavals of two world wars, the great depression of the 1930s, and the sparsity of publishers willing to risk her work? How to explain her enduring stature in the face of incomprehension? Her power is rooted in that "complex force of femininity" defined by Virginia Woolf in her 1929 work *A Room of One's Own*. Gertrude Stein is the great woman writer of the twentieth century that Virginia Woolf profiled for us. At the very least she had a room of her own, 500 pounds a year, and, one is tempted to add teasingly, a wife of her own.

Gertrude Stein was born at an interesting time, 1874, just after *Middlemarch* and before *Daniel Deronda,* just after George Eliot had perfected the form of the English novel and just before she started to take it apart. Like all great writers Gertrude Stein had a clear sense of the work that had been completed and of what remained to be done. By her birth the great English domestic novel had been perfected. By the time she reached maturity as a writer the first great wave of Western feminism had spent itself with the acquisition of the vote.

The first two decades of the twentieth century were for Stein a period of enormous productivity. The shape of that period can be traced through an examination of three major works: *Three Lives, The Making of Americans,* and *Tender Buttons.* During this period she established herself as an expatriate American woman living in France, and confirmed her lesbian identity as a comfortable and communal part of her life. It is important not only that Alice replaced her brother Leo as the central person in her life beyond herself, but that she and Alice surrounded themselves with a circle of friends which grew over the years to include artists, writers, dilettantes, and bureaucrats—a pleasant sampling of the bohemian, traditional, homosexual, and heterosexual community.

During this period she cemented her lifelong friendship with Picasso. In 1906 they spent long sittings for the now famous portrait, spent them talking endlessly about art, form, and change. Who can say who influenced whom? Cubism was born after "Melanctha," *Tender Buttons* after the famous portrait of Gertrude Stein—with its twice-done face that looks so hauntingly like Picasso's own. That portrait, Stein says, "how it came about they do not know. Picasso had never had anybody pose for him since he was sixteen years old, he was then twenty-four and Gertrude Stein had never thought of having her portrait painted, and they do not either of them know how it came about. Anyway it did and she posed to him for this portrait ninety times and a great deal happened during that time." [1]

With characteristic understatement, Stein thus introduces the motif of literary and artistic influence, evolution, and creativity. She continues: "It had been a fruitful winter. In the long struggle with the portrait of Gertrude Stein, Picasso passed from the Harlequin, the charming early Italian period to the intensive struggle which was to end in cubism. Gertrude Stein had written the story of Melanctha the negress, the second story of *Three Lives* which was the first definite step away from the nineteenth century and into the twentieth century in literature." [2]

In *Three Lives* Stein established her mastery of the novella, much as Mondrian began his career with exquisite representational art. With *The Making of Americans,* Stein pushed to its limits the bourgeois novel of the family, treating the form appropriately as a celebration of national as well as familial values, each character treated flatly as having equal value, the ultimate expression of the democratic ideal, a society of individuals, each of equal interest. In *Tender Buttons* all the passion, intellect, and sensuality implicit in the feminist movement then dominant in Germany, America, England, and to a more limited extent France, burst through in a statement of metaphysical complexity.

It is important to understand the source of Gertrude Stein's self-confidence and composure. She was the child of the first great wave of feminism, not its mother. Because those women cut the path she was free to be a writer. At the end of her life she paid tribute to Susan B. Anthony with a grandness that underscores her awareness of her heritage. She might have said of the political activities of Crystal Eastman, Emma Goldman, the Pankhurst women, and all the others, as she said of herself and Picasso: "When you make a thing, it is so complicated making it that it is bound to be ugly, but those that do it after you don't have to worry about making it and they can make it pretty." [3]

Other women were busy creating the political, social, and professional milieu within which Stein wrote. This is the meaning of her famous passage about feminism in *The Autobiography of Alice B. Toklas—* inevitably quoted out of context. Stein was failing her way out of the Johns Hopkins Medical School, and a feminist friend admonished her to button up her shoes and succeed. "There was great excitement in the medical school. Her very close friend Marion Walker pleaded with her, she said, but Gertrude, Gertrude remember the cause of women, and Gertrude Stein said, you don't know what it is to be bored." [4] It is not that Stein was not a feminist, but that, as she writes a few paragraphs later, "the cause of women or any other cause . . . does not happen to be her business." [5] Stein rested comfortably and knowingly in the bosom of the movement these women were creating and did her writing, which was her business.

Stein's most serious contribution may be in her challenge to gender as a significant category in human experience. In this perception she was very radical. Cocteau in the teens announced that Stein had freed his generation. Reading the manuscript of *Tender Buttons,* he was overcome by the statement "Dining is west." In the 1920s Virgil Thomson joined her in fruitful collaboration. These were artists who themselves treated gender cavalierly.

That the greatest lesbian feminist writer of her day should so persistently be treated as Picasso's artistic half-sister and Hemingway's literary mother tells us something of the lengths that patriarchal criticism will go to obscure the issues. Stein wrote about human nature and the human mind, and her point of view was philosophic, as befitted a student of Santayana and William James and a friend of Alfred North Whitehead. She was interested in character and in the functioning of the mind, and was truly radical in her belief that gender is meaningless: "I think nothing about men and women because that has nothing to do with anything. Anybody who is an American can know anything about this thing." [6] That there are men and women is demonstrable, but that it means nothing is not. This conviction that the human mind is without gender, combined with her historical sense that the twentieth century is a period of confusion, gave her the supreme confidence to create her art over the period of some forty years during which she was ignored or trivialized by the professional literary establishment.

Stein shared with Virginia Woolf the sense that masculinity has gotten out of hand in the twentieth century. Woolf, clinging to her somewhat fanciful notion that the androgynous mind has a masculine and feminine side, says:

> Virility has now become self-conscious—men, that is to say, are now writing only with the male side of their brains. It is a mistake for a woman to read them, for she will inevitably look for something that she will not find . . . some of the finest works of our greatest living writers fall upon deaf ears. Do what she will a woman cannot find in them that fountain of perpetual life which the critics assure her is there. It is not only that they celebrate male virtues, enforce male values and describe the world of men; it is that the emotion with which these books are permeated is to a woman incomprehensible. . . . The fact is that neither Mr. Galsworthy nor Mr. Kipling has a spark of the woman in him. Thus all their qualities seem to a woman, if one may generalize, crude and immature. They lack suggestive power. [7]

Writing in 1936 Stein reported a conversation focusing on the issue of confidence:

> I said to [Dashiell] Hammett there is something that is puzzling. In the nineteenth century the men when they were writing did invent all kinds and a great number of men. The women on the other hand never could invent women they always made the women be themselves seen splendidly or sadly or heroically or beautifully or despairingly or gently, and they never could make any other kind of woman. From Charlotte Brontë to George Eliot and many years later this was true. Now in the twentieth century it is the men who do it. The men all write about themselves, they are always themselves as strong or weak or mysterious or passionate or drunk or controlled but always themselves as the women used to do in the nineteenth century. Now you yourself always do it now why is it. He said it's simple. In the nineteenth century the men were confident, the women were not but in the twentieth century the men have no confidence and so they have to make themselves as you say more beautiful more intriguing more everything and they cannot make any other man because they have to hold on to themselves not having any confidence.[8]

Therein lies the secret of Stein's impact on three generations. She had confidence when men had lost theirs and women had not yet gotten theirs.

Another of Stein's vital contributions to twentieth-century literature is to challenge the authority of myth. By the 1920s Stein had identified herself and Joyce as the major writers of the period. The significant literary relation of that decade in Paris was between Stein and Joyce—who scarcely ever met, though half of Paris sat at their feet on alternate weeks: he the ex-Catholic master of myth and she the Jew who chose to look strictly at the fact. In a sense *Four Saints in Three Acts* is about herself and Joyce. There are in St. Theresa and St. Ignatius two central figures, separate, equal, parallel, and fundamentally different. Here, as in her relation with her brother Leo, the central ideal comes to be one of comparison and contrast, not of polarity.

Stein asserted that she was a modernist as Joyce was not. Her statement is important, for she was not an influence in any conventional sense on Pound, T.S. Eliot, and Joyce, the most important expatriate writers. The essence of her style, verbal experiments aside, is that she does not use myth. Joyce is magnificent in his rebellion against the church and nation, but it never occurred to him to question patriarchy or the myths that perpetuate it. As Joyce sought to fly the nets of state and religion, so Stein's concern was to fly the net of myth and with it of gender. Hilda Doolittle was more traditional in her literary strategies and took the risky route of rewriting myth, as in *Helen of Egypt*. Stein did not. By avoiding myth and plot in the conventional Aristotelian sense, Stein freed herself to ignore patriarchal values and gender-defined relations. In contrast, Virginia Woolf's commitment to realism and a narrative voice forced her, as it did Joyce, into a presentation of the sexes as they conventionally experience themselves, not as seen by a gender-free eye from another planet or future age. By refusing to engage in plots, by treating types rather than genders, by writing metaphysical rather than dramatic poetry, and by doing portraits and theater rather than narrative, Stein escaped stylistically the net of gender. Each moment is as it is, not as the patriarchs would have us see it. No wonder she delighted and liberated Cocteau, Van Vechten, and Thomson, even when they could not always fathom the complex force of her femininity.

It is appropriate to turn to Stein herself for her own sense of self during the 1920s. *Four Saints in Three Acts* was written in 1927 at the same time as "Patriarchal Poetry," and just before Virginia Woolf's *Orlando* and *A Room of One's Own*. She sets out "to tease a saint seriously," and the saints she teases are herself and Joyce. *Four Saints* is central to our understanding of what she thought she was doing by the 1920s. Far from being a stylistic tour de force, form without content, it is a straightforward account of two artists alive and well in Paris. They are surrounded by other artists and aspiring souls (or, rather, artists and dilettantes). St. Theresa, with overtones of George Eliot and *Middlemarch*, is seated beatifically half inside and outside the garden of contemplation, surrounded by nuns singing gaily. In many ways the vision is as funny as anything in Djuna Barnes' *Ladies' Almanack*. The center of the play is a sort of mass with the trappings of Easter, a playful exploration of Joyce's method, just as the resounding "fact" with which the opera ends is a statement of her own philosophy and method. In its vision and modality it is closer to the work of Florine Stettheimer, the fluidity and grace of Virginia Woolf, or the world of Natalie Barney than to the manly world of Hemingway and Faulkner, or the culturally weighty world of Eliot and Pound. Among the Americans only Wallace Stevens has the same quality.

It is hard to talk about Gertrude Stein in the same terms that one discusses the figures most commonly associated with the 1920s. Older than most, raised in America during the ascendancy of the nineteenth-century feminists, the themes most commonly used to organize the experience of the expatriate generation do not work for her. She had left her homeland for good, as they in the main had not; she still rejoiced in it in a patriotic fashion; and the great war had not left her shattered, disillusioned, or alienated. To the contrary, she had done some of her most original work during the war years. It was the period of her erotic poetry, which grew directly out of the sensual work of the prewar period. It is inappropriate to talk of a woman of forty-six as losing her innocence in the great war. She was no sheltered spinster. She was a lesbian writer living in Montmartre. She shrugged her shoulders much as she would have us believe the French shrugged theirs.

It was good for Gertrude Stein that she had a rich sex life, a comfortable domestic establishment, and a wide circle of cosmopolitan friends, but it makes it hard to fit her into the more conventional studies focused on the experience of young men born near the turn of the century. Her identity crisis had come in the first decade of the century and had focused on her assertion, in the face of male disinterest and disapprobation, that she was a serious writer. The story of her struggle is carefully chronicled in "Patriarchal Poetry," written in 1927. The experience and themes laid out there, while they may speak to the condition of women artists in the nineteenth and twentieth centuries, are not the themes of Joyce, T.S. Eliot, Hemingway, Frost, Stevens, and Faulkner, though she shared with her male compatriots the search for a modern voice. What was remarkable was her conviction that she spoke for all of them. As she says in *The Geographical History of America:* "It is natural that again a woman should be the one to do the literary thinking of this epoch." [9] The voice that emerges is authorial without being masculine, and the pattern of mind traced owes nothing to patriarchal myth.

As Stein says: "There are of course people who are more important than others in that they have more importance in the world, but this is not essential, and it ceases to be. . . . Just as everybody has the vote, including the women, I think children should, because as soon as a child is conscious of itself, then it has to me an existence and has a stake in what happens." [10] Joyce thought history a nightmare from which one awakens, but sadly he awakened into patriarchal myth. Stein willingly abandoned plot, conventional narrative strategies, generic solutions, myth, and stock characters. She had to do all this if she as a woman was to convey accurately and compellingly her experience as a human being. In our generation feminist scholars and critics are increasingly turning to women's diaries, journals, and letters in their attempt to find the authentic voice of women, undistorted to meet the preconceptions of patriarchal teachers, editors, and publishers. Being a woman, a lesbian, and a Jew, Stein could not afford traditional stories and stock characters. She had to focus on fact and not fabrication.

The confusion manifested by so many fine readers of Stein is a combination of being moved by the work, yet unable to admit its truth. Just as Virgil Thomson refuses to understand "Patriarchal Poetry," so John Malcolm Brinnin wrote: "In only a minimal sense do typical plays of Gertrude Stein refer to anything. Yet while they are not 'about' anything, they insist on being something—and that 'thing' is Gertrude Stein's own, an almost improbable mixture of primitive mindlessness and sophisticated intellect. . . . Their sophistication lies in the fact that, without being ideological, they are always conceptual, always based in a governing idea even though that idea may be all but dissolved in the presentation." [11] Thomson's and Brinnin's responses suggest how hard it has been for even the most sympathetic supporters to attend to the authentic voice of this twentieth-century woman.

The twenties were not a major period for Stein; it was as if she was resting from the labors of the first two decades in preparation for the work of the 1930s. In fact, in terms of feminist scholarship, the 1920s may well emerge as the beginning of a long decline rather than a moment of artistic glory. Women had gained the right to vote, to be clerical workers, to be flappers, and to be sexually available to men. But the major English-language writers of the period were not interested in the emancipation of women—quite the opposite.

By the late 1920s the great patriarchal reaction had set in. In the early 1930s the internationally renowned homosexual library in Berlin at the Institute for Sexual Science was burned—10,000 volumes into the flames. Even as early as 1928, Radclyffe Hall was under serious attack, and there were other signs that "the quality of life" was declining. In the face of these repressive measures, the banning of the *Well of Loneliness* may be more significant than the banning of *Ulysses*. The former, representing the tip of the homosexual iceberg, offered a far more profound challenge to the existing order than *Ulysses,* which remains a profoundly Catholic and therefore traditional novel.

Periodization in literary history focusing on the 1920s as a period of great significance sheds little light on Stein's career. Her period of high creativity was prewar, with the 1930s marking her next most serious work. The 1920s may have been a time of sexual liberation for heterosexuals; one can argue as persuasively that in the final decade of the nineteenth century and the first two of the twentieth gender was being challenged as a ruling concept and that by the 1920s there was the beginning of a serious return to traditional roles, albeit with freer heterosexual behavior.

Stein focused on different phenomena than most of her contemporary fellow writers. This difference has great significance for how we treat the question of influence and especially periodization in terms of the stature, impact, and contribution of women writers in American literature. One ends with the serious question of what constitutes a period in the work of Gertrude Stein. Serious feminist creativity had spent itself by the teens, and the vote, though gained, represented a narrowing of focus within the movement. The most significant breakthroughs before the 1920s had come in America—where anything could be thought about men and women. The same thing happened in England and on the continent, but America, with its spaces, shallower civilization, and its commitment to individualism and democracy, was quicker to actualize new behavior for women. It may well be, as T.S. Eliot said in his maturity, that humankind cannot bear too much reality; and that the devastation of the first great war, the frenzy of the interwar period, and the machinelike dehumanization of the second great war, will appear to future historians as the convulsions of a patriarchal civilization confronted from within by the growth of feminist and humanitarian consciousness. As Gertrude Stein might have said, "We am interested."

NOTES

1. Gertrude Stein, *The Autobiography of Alice B. Toklas* (1933; New York: Vintage, 1960), pp. 45 ff.
2. Ibid., p. 45.
3. Ibid., p. 23.
4. Ibid., p. 82.
5. Ibid., p. 83.
6. Gertrude Stein, *The Geographical History of America* (1936; New York: Vintage, 1973), p. 214.
7. Virginia Woolf, *A Room of One's Own* (1929; New York: Harcourt, Brace, & World, 1957), pp. 105 ff.
8. Gertrude Stein, *Everybody's Autobiography* (1937; New York: Vintage, 1973), p. 5.
9. *Geographical History of America*, p. 228.
10. Gertrude Stein, "A Transatlantic Interview, 1946." In *A Primer for the Gradual Understanding of Gertrude Stein*, ed. Robert Bartlett Haas (Los Angeles: Black Sparrow, 1971), pp. 16 ff.
11. Gertrude Stein, *Selected Operas and Plays of Gertrude Stein*, ed. John Malcolm Brinnin (Pittsburgh: University of Pittsburgh Press, 1970), p. xiii.

PART II
Women Writers and Artists

Introduction

Paris in the twenties was the center of creative talent. Writers, musicians, painters, and sculptors came from around the world hoping to blossom in its propitious intellectual climate. American artists who left for Paris commonly referred to themselves as expatriates and frequently went to the City of Light to be among other American writers and write about home. This literary generation of cultural expatriates, which included Djuna Barnes, E.E. Cummings, Ernest Hemingway, Ezra Pound, and Gertrude Stein, among many others, believed that society, in the sense of "good company," could not be found in the United States. If it existed anywhere, it existed in the Paris of the twenties.

Not all American artists could afford or wished to travel to Paris. For those who remained, the most consistently attractive haven was Greenwich Village or, if you were Black, Harlem. These enclaves protected those who lived there from the vulgarization of city life. These were the places where young men and women from small towns and prairie states could forget middle-class manners and customs and create something new. Although popular among artists, the Village could not compare with the stimulation and excitement of the Left Bank.

Paris and New York were particularly congenial for the development of women's talents as writers and artists or as sponsors of the talented. Like their male counterparts, they sought a second home where they could find a freer, fuller, and more satisfying intellectual life from which to examine American life and values and their own inner feelings. In the first article of this section Maureen Howard examines the personal geography or inner being of five prominent women authors as compared with the geographic city, either Paris or New York, in which they lived and worked. Each writer—Edith Wharton, Gertrude Stein, Edna St. Vincent Millay, Marianne Moore, and Willa Cather—used her city as a backdrop for her novels or poems, but each also transcended her locale for another city, that of her imagination and words—the city where she "lived." The latter, Howard finds, is infinitely more interesting than any description of actual environment.

The important influence of the inner self is also the subject of the chapter by Sara Via Pais. Women of the twenties, drawn from childhood into the nets of others' needs and definitions, were often urged to curb the individual and the artist to family, community, and society. Pais reflects on the ways some women overcame the repression of the social self and shaped elements of their self-awareness and experience into poems, paintings, and other works. As examples of women involved in conscious self-cultivation, she examines the statements and artistic creations of Louise Nevelson, Georgia O'Keeffe, and Djuna Barnes, a sculptor, painter, and writer, respectively. The 1920s gave us the first generation of women artists who explored not just their geographic surroundings but their own landscapes of body and mind.

Although somewhat younger, Emily Hahn has known personally many of the writers of the 1920s. In her essay "Salonists and Chroniclers," she takes a personal look at the lives and works of three prominent women—Natalie Barney, Mabel Dodge Luhan, and Janet Flanner. The first two were best known as celebrated hostesses of the Left Bank rather than for the books they published. As salonists they served as catalytic agents, mixing their friends from the worlds of art and literature and sampling the results with relish. The third was known for her writings, most notably her fortnightly "Letter from Paris" published in *The New Yorker* for thirty-five years under her pen name, Genêt. She was not merely writing a letter all those years but interpreting the nation of France to the American people.

In the evolution of literature, as Janet Flanner once stated, the book publisher has been the second essential factor. Individually, the publisher has rarely gained fame as the necessary element connected with the appearance of a new great book. This was not true of the private publishers of Paris. As Hugh Ford points out, they found their permanent niche in literary history by being remarkable midwives to a generation of remarkable genius. Ford examines the roles played by six women publishers—Sylvia Beach, Margaret Anderson, Jane Heap,

Nancy Cunard, Barbara Harrison, and Caresse Crosby. The history of their small presses is as diverse as the women themselves. Jointly, their intuition, innovation, toil, and willingness to take risks produced books and journals that would influence generations to come.

Black presence in the New York of the 1920s was more visible than ever before; so much so that Black artists proclaimed a renaissance. In the final article in this section, Cheryl Wall examines the personal lives and writings of a number of Black women poets and novelists. Doubly oppressed, Wall states, Black women writers were highly aware of the degrading stereotypes of mammy, mulatto, and whore commonly applied to them. As a result, certain subjects in their writings, particularly sex, were taboo and the language, more often than not, genteel. Most hesitated to use the themes or language of their heritage and, when they did, they often constructed an idealized portrait of Blacks as intelligent, cultured, noble, and respectable. This portrait was as distorted as the negative portrayals it attempted to displace. There were some exceptions, notably the blues singers, as illustrated through the verse of Bessie Smith and author Zora Neale Hurston. Their work is born from Black folk life—their language and references immediately define them as Black and Southern. The women portrayed in their works had independence, inner strength, and common sense. Smith and Hurston, Wall explains, were the "signifiers" who broke the psychological chains that permitted Black women in literature to begin to be themselves.

5.

City of Words

Maureen Howard

Omissions are deliberate.
Marianne Moore

Gertrude Stein said "remarks are not literature" to Hemingway, a remark she found worth repeating twice in the same book. She said he was ninety percent Rotarian, looked like a Spaniard. On the wave of her first big success, before departing for America, she bought a mink coat, and so did Willa Cather in the wake of a best seller. That one time Fitzgerald was taken to visit Edith Wharton at the Pavillon Colombe, he came drunk. As her farewell, before she sailed for France, Vincent Millay, as she was known, sat on her day bed in Greenwich Village and directed Edmund Wilson and John Peale Bishop to make love to her, assigning Wilson to her lower half while Bishop got above the waist—this incident presumably throwing new light upon her famous lines: "My candle burns at both ends/ It will not hold the night."

Well, we must be careful not to gossip. All the special moments, the brilliant exchanges, the Poiret hat ornaments, early touring cars, middy blouses, menus, the miniature armchair done in petit point by Miss Toklas according to the design of Braque, Picasso, whoever—and the love affairs, yes, even the love affairs become artifacts. We seem to derive such comfort handling them, knowing their surfaces in detail as though fifty years later some of the charm will rub off on us, or maybe even some of the genius.

Paris and New York—the magic decade. If we open the chic coffee table book, we find between the views of Barrow Street, Washington Square Arch, Café du Dome, and the salon at 27 rue de Fleurus, a strange personal geography infinitely more interesting than the old artistic photos. Edith Wharton, Gertrude Stein, Edna St. Vincent Millay, Marianne Moore, Willa Cather—each was extraordinarily conscious of place, used her city, and in all cases but one, transcended in their work any of the usual ideas we may have about the Paris and New York of expatriate writing.

In 1920 Edith Wharton published *The Age of Innocence*. In one sense it is an historical novel, an attempt to recapture New York society circa 1880-1905, but for Wharton, who had been living and writing in France for so many years, it was a final acceptance of her American heritage. In speaking of a group of religious bohemians, her heroine, Madame Olenska, says:

> But do you know, they interest me much more than the blind conformity to tradition—somebody else's tradition—that I see among our own friends. It seems stupid to have discovered America only to make it into a copy of another country. . . . Do you suppose Christopher Columbus would have taken all that trouble just to go to the opera with the Selfridge Merrys? [1]

The question is amusing yet difficult, and Wharton's hero, Newland Archer, answers it with the rest of his life, an American life that finds its own values, its own originality, even its own freedom within the walls of his library. Paris is a beautiful stage set at the end of the novel, a lush, romantic Paris as Archer sees it, with "the life of art and study and pleasure that filled each mighty artery to bursting." It is a vision that Archer rejects in favor of a validation of his own choices, his own life. Wharton loved France, lived comfortably and freely there—dealing with her America from a distance in novel after novel. Remembering it all. But there was still another place where she lived. In her autobiography, *A Backward Glance*, she names it "The Secret Garden," a coy title, yet it is the only decent chapter in a fraudulent work. It is about her professional life, which she here calls her "real life"—a place where she experiences "great emotional excitement, quite unrelated to the joy or sorrow caused by real happenings, but as intense, and with as great an appearance of reality." [2]

Wharton's secret garden bears a remarkable resemblance to the following bit of Steinian geography:

> After all everybody, that is, everybody who writes is interested in living inside themselves in order to tell what is inside themselves. That is why writers have to have two countries, the one where they belong and the one in which they live really. The second one is romantic, it is separate from themselves, it is not real but it is really there.[3]

One of Gertrude Stein's statements, absolutely clear, so apparent in its good reason that she begins with "after all." For Stein the interior country held her first allegiance, so that her actual countries, America and France, created no problems she could not solve. She was always fascinated by her Americanism. "America is my country and Paris is my hometown," she proclaimed happily in a late work, *Paris, France.* For forty-five years she read and spoke French badly. Paris provided the perfect setting in which she could establish a loving isolation with what she called "her english," a city in which she could "live really," where she could fully enjoy and recreate the simplicities of English grammar.

Paris was her city of words. Apart from the theory she tossed around with cubists and surrealists, apart from the personal freedom of style Paris offered—Stein needed France to keep her native language peculiar, immediate, always interesting to her. In *The Making of Americans,* published in 1925, a thousand pages of English words flowed out of her in a history, a grand folly. "I write for myself and others," it begins. I cannot help but feel her audience thins out, or cuts in and out of this impossibly self-indulgent work. But her writings, from the miniaturism of a complete picture of a word which she accomplishes in *Tender Buttons,* to the thoroughly accessible, moving narratives of World War II, *Brewsie and Willie* and *Paris, France,* are a history of the English language as she experienced it.

In a broader, more ordinary (for her) perception:

> The reason why all of us naturally began to live in France is because France has scientific methods, machines, and electricity, but does not really believe that these things have anything to do with the real business of living. Life is tradition and human nature. And so in the beginning of the Twentieth Century when a new way had to be found, naturally we needed France.[4]

The sense of reality she claimed for France made possible the modern temperament: it left the artist free to have the emotion of unreality. It is exhilarating to follow Stein's quirky one-way arguments that she always wins. In *Paris, France,* written at the outset of World War II, her feeling for her adopted "hometown" is so complete, her American language so authentic, that she becomes a citizen of both countries.

Edna St. Vincent Millay used up cities. *Her* New York, *her* Paris were backdrops for an aesthetic performance. The Village of legend: late parties, bathroom down the hall, embroidered Spanish shawls, free love, booze. With the publication of *Renascence,* her first book of poems, Millay became more than a literary success. She was a star. Self-consciously free, her spirit of the modern with its promiscuity and smart cynicism now seems dated. Look at this petulant poem called "Thursday":

> *And why you come complaining*
> *Is more than I can see.*
>
> *I loved you Wednesday, yes,*
> *But what is that to me.*[5]

Or this narcissistic line by the reigning beauty of bohemia: "The unremembered lads/ Who turned to me at midnight with a sigh." A faint decadence was combined with an idealization of art: "Euclid Alone Has Looked on Beauty Bare/ O blinding hour, O holy terrible Day/ When first the shaft into his vision shone/ Of light anatomized." Her fluent verse is all from other centuries and now rings as entirely too literary, the emotion floating on the surface like her rhymes.

It is legitimate to gossip about Millay; she would have liked it—as a successful New York career girl, under the name of Nancy Boyd, she wrote clever poems and occasional pieces for Mencken and Nathan's *Smart Set,* but preserved her real name as though the popular strain would contaminate the high art of her lyric poetry. When she exhausted New York she went to Europe. When she exhausted Europe she came back to New York. It was 1923, the year in which Gertrude Atherton explains to us in her New York novel: "The village was once a colony of artists, but the big fish left and the minnows swim slimily about, giving off nothing but their own sickly phosphorescence." With the instincts of a true showman, Vincent Millay knew when to quit. Worn down but still intense, she married and soon left the city. But she needed an audience and toured America reading her poems, always performing in a flowing gown somewhat too long, like the one she had borrowed from a rich woman for her first reading—that had worked—the fragile poor girl, stylish waif. She believed her role fully. Quite apart from her poems, she was our "poetess." Unlike Stein, she could not survive her era or her celebrity.

Once and only once, in 1911, Marianne Moore went to Paris with her mother. They stayed in a hotel on the Left Bank and on a memorably hot night they walked to 12, rue de l'Odéon, to see Sylvia Beach's

Shakespeare & Company Bookshop. Miss Moore said: "It wouldn't occur to me to say, 'Here am I. I'm a writer, would you talk to me awhile?' I had no feeling at all like that. I wanted to observe things." No idle compliments from strangers nor further tours were necessary. She was a New Yorker. She saw everything about her with great accuracy and discrimination. *Genuine*—that is a word she often used. She wanted her poetry to be genuine. In the twenties in Greenwich Village, with all the standard bohemians pushing to be original, Marianne Moore's originality was effortless. In a world that had begun to proliferate with things, a century of manufactured things, she insisted upon the exactness of the object seen, a magical naming, coupled with the restraint of her defining. Yet her poetry could be open, unreserved at times—Whitmanesque—with a stately rhetoric. The poem "New York" (from *Observations,* published in 1924) is a local history and a short American history. It refers to our primitive past when New York was the center of fur trade. It sets us apart from the European market. But Moore gives us that lush romantic lore only to take it away again. The past cannot contain the New York she wants us to see, nor will she allow us to be mere tourists or purveyors:

> *It is not the dime-novel exterior,*
> *Niagara Falls, the calico horses and the war-canoe;*
> *it is not that 'if the fur is not finer than such as one sees others wear,*
> *one would rather be without it'—*
> *that estimated in raw meat and berries, we could feed the universe;*
> *it is not the atmosphere of ingenuity.*[6]

Neither the museums nor Seventh Avenue make up Marianne Moore's city. She turns in the final line to a phrase of Henry James—"accessibility to experience," at last defining not only her New York but what may be America's best hope.

Willa Cather worked in Pittsburgh and New York as a teacher, journalist, and editor. Cities were a necessity for her, a hard fact, as they were for so many of the writers and musicians who appear in her fiction. Dangerous and beautiful urban landscapes appear in her work holding out the promise of fame, fortune, and inevitable heartbreak. Cather knew what the artist must give up—the security of friendship, family life, the limits of a town in which you know where the sidewalks end. Grueling long days in the office of *McClure's Magazine* is what Cather knew in New York City, but she also knew that the glamor, the anonymity, the theatricality of this city was as necessary to her as cash. To Lucy Gayheart, the most autobiographical of Willa Cather's heroines, the city is "where the air trembled like a tuning fork with unimaginable possibilities. . . . The city of feeling rose out of the city of fact."

It is not surprising to find in one of Cather's few personal memoirs that she could stage a bit of an entrance, appearing somewhat late to a dinner in her honor at Delmonico's in a gown of rich claret velvet. But in the deepest sense she knew how to resist the dazzle. In speaking of her life as an artist Cather wrote: "Life began for me when I ceased to admire and began to remember."

UPDATED VIEW

When I came back to live in Greenwich Village in 1966, Marianne Moore lived around the block. At first she walked out, sprightly in her cape and legendary tricorn hat. Each time it was wonderful to see her—she became quite real, more an aspect of the neighborhood than a link with a literary past. Then she walked out with a young companion. Then not at all. Next the obituary in the *Times*. She had won all the prizes. Her death notice looped back as death notices will, to the grand old days at the *Dial*, the heyday of Greenwich Village, and I remembered then, reading of her old associates and haunts, a party I had been invited to years before when I was fresh out of college, invited by Oscar Williams, the anthologist and poet—a party in a loft down on Water Street, before anyone thought of living in advertised lofts. But they had. Oscar and his poetess wife, Gene Durwood. There they were, a roomful, drinking, talking on into the night. "We moderns" in their sixties, with ascots, arty scarves, long earrings and sandals—ashen people, threadbare every one, still proclaiming their individuality and about to vote for Adlai Stevenson with all the passionate conviction they had had for Eugene Debs. With the exception of Louise Bogan, they were all "minnows," only too glad to talk about the old days when poets and painters appeared at every street corner. Reginald Marsh climbed the arch in Washington Square on an "all-night drunk" and some no-account tourist trap stood in place of the Provincetown Playhouse. It was all terribly disheartening, their dry myth. I'll never forget it—the twenties in the Village gone stale. The lesson can only be to look up from the narrow streets, out at a new landscape—to the pillar of light caught between the twin towers of the World Trade Center on a bright morning and at night to the new disco lighting, vulgar and exciting, that flashes off the spire of the Empire State.

NOTES

1. Edith Wharton, *The Age of Innocence* (New York: Appleton, 1920), p. 205.
2. Edith Wharton, *A Backward Glance* (New York: Appleton, 1934), p. 242.

3. Gertrude Stein, *Paris France* (New York: Charles Scribner's Sons, 1940), p. 2.
4. Ibid., p. 8.
5. Edna St. Vincent Millay, *A Few Figs from Thistles: Poems and Sonnets* (New York: Frank Shay, 1921), p. 10
6. Marianne Moore, *Observations* (New York: Dial Press, 1924), p. 65.

6.

Shapes of the Feminine Experience in Art

Sara Via Pais

What then is to be done with a woman
Who must be alone to
Feel and who being left alone is
Pleased with herself past.

Ernest Walsh, 1925

In retrospect, it all seems fresh, exciting, and easy—the myth of the poster girl, Miss Liberty in an art deco ensemble. What could have been more inspiring, more liberating, than American artistic life in the twenties, focusing as it did first on Greenwich Village, that part of New York that bears the name of the place where time begins, and having its last outpost on Montparnasse, the mountain of the gods, in Paris? When, in the short history of American arts and letters, had life and art come so close to each other, when had style been such a preoccupation in both domains?

Although there is the assumption of a meaningful link between life and art, we are uncertain as to how to articulate it; unlike James Joyce, who was once gently reminded by a well-meaning friend that life and art are not the same thing—to which Joyce firmly replied that if they were not, they ought to be.

I cannot presume to explore the deep relationships between lived experience and its ultimate transformation into art, but I would like to

49

share some reflections on the ways certain women artists of the twenties shaped elements of their experience into the poems, paintings, and texts they created. Our focus on this subject confirms that their lives and works have in some way given form and direction to our own. As a first approach let me quote a poem by Louise Bogan, one of the finest poets and critics working in the twenties. In this sonnet she articulates some of the ideas essential to understanding the trajectory of the lives and works of her sister artists, however disparate they may otherwise seem.

> *Since you would claim the sources of my thought*
> *Recall the meshes whence it sprang unlimed,*
> *The reedy traps which other hands have timed*
> *To close upon it. Conjure up the hot*
> *Blaze that it cleared so cleanly, or the snow*
> *Devised to strike it down. It will be free.*
> *Whatever nets draw in to prison me*
> *At length your eyes must turn to watch it go.*
> *My mouth, perhaps, may learn one thing too well,*
> *My body hear no echo save its own,*
> *Yet will the desperate mind, maddened and proud,*
> *Seek out the storm, escape the bitter spell*
> *That we obey, strain to the wind, be thrown*
> *Straight to its freedom in the thunderous cloud.*[1]

   The first key is in Bogan's direction to seek the sources of thought in experience, for thought springs into being from the encounter between the self and events and experiences that produce self-awareness. For Bogan, as a woman artist, these encounters are seen as meshes, traps, nets. A woman first, she is drawn from childhood into the nets of others' needs and definitions; she is urged to curb the passionate "I" and learn to say "we"—to place the "I" of the individual and artist after the "we" of family, community, society. But in Bogan's language the self has wings and no fear of flying; while the objects that represent impediments to that flight are figured as earthbound: meshes, traps, intemperate climes. The conflict is clear; but so is the sense that the will and energy of the self are released by brushes with entrapment, and that a necessary tension exists between the "desperate mind, maddened and proud," and the things that menace it. For they do not only threaten, they also galvanize. In reaction to them the self is flung into freedom. And in the poem's final line, we understand that flight is not escape, it is esthetic distance. The poet's experience has become poetry, the private struggles have assumed visible shape, and our eyes "turn to watch it go."

In this poem, as in the lives and works of the women we celebrate here, there is a powerful impression of will and energy bursting out, a sense of something new in American artistic life: the twenties gave us the first generation of women artists who came out of the closets, attics, and parlors where lady artists had long been consigned to covering the notebook with their needlework. This is the first generation of American women to openly share a commitment to the enterprise of art, the first generation able to demand and create full and expressive lives from which to generate that art.

They did not come to that extraordinary moment unaided. They were able to build their work upon the series of gradual artistic emancipations won by their esthetic foremothers; and they were daughters of strong, independent, self-willed women. Recent research into the formation of the female psyche shows what we can intuitively learn from the lives of Janet Flanner, Djuna Barnes, Kay Boyle, Willa Cather and others like them: there is expressive power available to the woman who has seen the qualities of courage, curiosity, and pride confirmed as womanly in the first person she loves—her mother.

Bogan's poem is also about the struggle between the individual and social self. An artist lives and works out of the individual self, but growing up female has traditionally meant learning to repress the one in favor of the other. Women artists of earlier times have had to bury the individual self under the social self, showing its passive-impassive face to the world. Those who could not quite manage the juggling act could still be neatly confined within the verdict of insanity.

Women artists of the twenties show us what it is to let the individual self rule the shaping of the social self. They refuse to take on the protective coloration of outward conformity; they will not secrete themselves or their work behind the façade of tidy lives. They are marvelously visible, audible, and they please themselves. In that famous generation where men were lost, women artists were finding in themselves an intense self-awareness, powerful will, and the deeply American conviction that one can have it all—life and work.

Behind all this was the belief that liberation of the mind is not enough; liberation of the whole person had to be accomplished. These women believed in the vital connection between the person and her esthetic persona, which is one of the fundamental tenets of Romantic and post-Romantic art. In the modern world, art has become less a matter of representation of universals and more a personal expression of visions of the nature and order of things. *Experience* and *experiment* have the same root; and in French there is only one word, *expérience*, for the two activities. If art in the modern world is an expression of experience, its creation presupposes some sort of experimentation in the world.

To gain full access to the range of experience that nourishes creativity, women artists had to come into full contact with the world. They created for themselves lives not defined within social and sexual circumscriptions, allowing their own needs to shape their experience. It all looks easy at the safe distance of fifty years. But it was neither easy nor graceful. *Ulysses* was published in France and banned in America, while on the home front appeared two versions of American social reality: the ironic version was Sinclair Lewis' *Babbitt;* the straight one was Emily Post's *Etiquette.* Hypocrisy and repression are the stuff of which great novels are made, but only by artists who have distanced themselves from such experiences, who have flown free from those traps and nets.

"Desire is creation," wrote Willa Cather. Elsewhere she enlarged upon this notion: "Every artist makes [her]self born." [2] Out of desire, the artist creates a self which simultaneously embodies her in the world and marks her out as distinct, unassailably herself, unlike any other being. Such presence holds the encroaching world at bay, distances it, so that she occupies within an authentic self a kind of psychic free zone in which her work can be developed. Sometimes an artist can gain access to that necessary free space by "withdrawing" to a place that gives it to her: New York, perhaps, or Paris. For others, there are still other spaces in which she makes her life and work.

I would like to comment on three artists who share certain characteristics: Louise Nevelson, Georgia O'Keeffe, and Djuna Barnes—a sculptor, a painter, a writer. One is first struck by their particular beauty of person. Not mere loveliness, but real, powerful beauty, the kind that can come only from a vital relation of the individual to the social self. There is in each of these women a self-cultivation fundamental to the work they created. They attained that ideal state in which, as Yeats had it, we cannot know the dancer from the dance. They made towering sculptures, glorious pictures, unique and brilliant prose. They accomplished this by exploring not just New York, Paris, or New Mexico, but by beginning with an exploration of their own landscapes of body and mind.

Louise Nevelson was not yet a working artist in the twenties. To all eyes but her own, she was a young upper-middle class wife in New York who preferred her operatic lessons to tea and mah-jongg. Beginning with a way of making music out of her own body, she continued to cultivate her self through the arts at the same time that she was breaking out of a life she could no longer bear because she had not made it for herself. Study in drawing, painting, sculpture and dance followed in the late twenties, and in the early thirties she began to build the world of sculpture which is not yet completed today.

"I have created an empire," she explains, and "what I wear every day, the way I comb my hair, all has something to do with it; the way you live a life." [3] Her work is feminine because it emerges from her experience of herself as a woman in relation to space, mass, volume, and line. She is at the center of that empire, she is its informing principle, and she has become herself a sculptural object, making up her person out of an assemblage of the same kinds of objects she integrates into her sculpture. There is something wonderfully suggestive about seeing her today, the turbaned head rising out of her artful costumes and ringed with a necklace she has sculpted: symbolic confirmation of the fact that she is the center of her work.

Georgia O'Keeffe left New York for New Mexico, and a style quite opposite that of Nevelson's flamboyance. Her life is lived in the shapes, colors, and spatial configurations of the world she creates in her paintings: huge desert flowers, a bleached animal skull, mesas and valleys and folded hills. She could not have seen them in quite the way she has, had she not had the experience of another landscape, that of the woman's body. She has been not only a maker of art, but also a subject of it, in the hundreds of photographs of her face and body made in the twenties and early thirties by Alfred Steiglitz. That was the first stage in the transformation of her physical self into art, as her paintings are the second and definitive stage. Her work displays an exploration of the lines, folds, and masses of the female body seen in nature.

Djuna Barnes is more difficult to speak about than Nevelson and O'Keeffe, because her work is so hard to find. Most of her writings are out of print; only her most important novel, *Nightwood,* is currently available. As we move toward a serious critical analysis of the nature of feminine discourse, we will turn to Barnes' work as a series of crucial texts. *Nightwood* is a journey into the spaces of the female mind, in which Barnes is concerned with questions of temporal and spatial relationships and with the expressive possibilities of language as it signifies for a woman.

The difficult, elusive, yet highly elaborated and stylized forms of Barnes' writing has a fundamental connection to her sense of self in the world. She moved through Paris and New York in the twenties at a certain distance from her contemporaries, elegantly and idiosyncratically dressed with the same taste for the recherché, the brilliant, the privately significant that characterized her prose style. That she possessed a strong sense of her own style is made clear in a delicious anecdote recounted by Edmund Wilson. Djuna Barnes was displaying to Wilson's then-wife Mary Blair a particularly lovely nightgown she had bought in Paris. "Yes," she sighed, "and I spent an entire summer looking for a night to go with the nightgown." [4]

I wanted to end on that playful note because in our comments about the work of these and other artists we often neglect to remind ourselves that artistic creation is a form of expressive play. For the artist it is Protean play, constantly transforming life into art into life, giving order and meaning, but free of the rules and regulations dominating the world of systematized and alienating work. Every culture sets limits on the amount of play or leeway it will grant artists, and every artist plays in part with the givens of that culture. But the deep source of art is in the artist's own life, a private experience of the world. As Martha Graham succinctly put it, "I believe in the *one.*"

All great artists believe in the one, in their own powers and vision. We tend to see them standing above or apart from the artistic community. This is at best a partial perspective. At some point the artist seeks and finds community among other artists—not simply as a social animal looking for companionship after working hours, nor as a lonely soul in need of refuge from an indifferent or hostile world, but as an actor in the experimental theater of artistic community in the modern world. In that community the artist can live out with others the desire of creation; it constitutes a space or arena in which experiment and expressive play can go on in whatever mode seems to suit: antic, frantic, dramatic, ironic, or merely energetic. Artistic community is confirmed from the outside as well, by those of us who do not belong to it directly but who need to know it is there. If it is theatre, we are its audience; it draws us into that psychic free zone where moments of pure self are enacted, where human singularity is confirmed.

In the twenties, the theaters of artistic community were in Paris and New York—but not the Paris and New York we now see. The actors and actresses were young and in process; today they are neatly arranged in rows of bibliographies, catalogs, memoirs, and theses, and their experiences have become anecdotes or artifacts. Yet that is not all. Those places, those women, those works have touched and altered our own imaginative experience; they have brought us together and inspired new perspectives and ideas.

I think it would have made Gertrude Stein very happy to have the last word, and so she shall. This is a passage from her critical writings, a comment on four American authors. It speaks eloquently of why and how we care about the lives and works of these women: "They do not reflect life or describe life or embroider life or photograph life, they express life and to express life takes essential intelligence. Whether to express life is the most interesting thing to do or the most important thing to do, I do not know, but I do know it is the most permanent thing to do." [5]

NOTES

1. Louise Bogan, *Body of This Death* (New York: Robert MacBride, 1923), p. 30.
2. Willa Cather, *The Professor's House* (New York: Knopf, 1925), p. 67.
3. Arnold Glimcher, *Louise Nevelson* (New York: Praeger, 1972), p. 43.
4. Edmund Wilson, *The Twenties* (New York: Farrar, Straus, & Giroux, 1975), p. 109.
5. "A Stitch in Time Saves Nine. Birds of a Feather Flock Together. Chickens Come Home to Roost," *Ex Libris* (March 1925).

7.

Salonists and Chroniclers

Emily Hahn

Literature, even more than painting, is a bastion for women, the one field in which they cannot be put down merely on account of anatomy. Men have been quick to note and—at times—to resent this fact: Hawthorne's furious remark about "the damned mob of scribbling women" is proof of it, as is the criticism evoked by Mrs. Aphra Behn when, during the Restoration, she dared to make a success of play-wrighting. Apart from inevitable remarks deploring the "sensitivity" of female novelists and poets or, conversely, their lack thereof, nothing has stopped women from success in writing. The three women named in this essay have been successful writers in their various ways. Two of them were known, perhaps, from the parties they gave rather than the books they published. At first glance one wonders if the three were not chosen completely at random. It is like one of those quizzes in the Sunday papers: "Tell us what the following have in common: (a) Natalie Barney; (b) Mabel Dodge Luhan; (c) Janet Flanner."

The quiz-taker does not have to think long to reach one obvious answer: they were all American women who lived abroad. But even this is not so simple. Natalie Barney was the only one of the three to live abroad all her mature life; Mabel Dodge Luhan came back to the United States at about the time of World War I and thereafter made only fleeting visits to the Continent; Janet Flanner spent the remaining years of her life in New York. Still, they had more than these points in common. All elected to live abroad because America did not offer them the aspects of culture they wanted. Whereas Luhan and Flanner ultimately decided that America had changed enough to be bearable, Barney was satisfied to remain in the country whose language and customs she had made her own.

According to her biographer George Wickes, who published *The Amazon of Letters: The Life and Loves of Natalie Barney,*[1] Barney really had little choice: her formative years were very much influenced by France. She grew up at a time when her parents, like other rich Americans, chose to make Europe rather than America their playground. Though in the course of time they owned houses here and there along the Atlantic seaboard, especially in Washington, D.C., they were forever popping over to Paris or the Riviera or, somewhat less often, to London. Natalie was born in 1876, when travel of this casual sort was the best way, people thought, to prove their superiority to their neighbors who had less interest than they in music, painting, and foreign languages and literature. In fairness to Luhan and Barney it should be emphasized that they appreciated the things they sought and found in Europe.

Mabel Dodge Luhan was almost of an age with Natalie Barney: she was born in 1879, but I have been unable to find proof that they ever met. There were points of contact, however, which I shall examine. Janet Flanner was much younger. She was acquainted with Barney, and once told Wickes: "Miss Barney is a perfect example of an enchanting person not to write about," but was helpful to him nevertheless. The one obvious difference between Barney, Luhan, and Flanner is that the first two were rich amateurs and the third had always been a professional.

Natalie Barney came of an Ohio family that cared about civilized culture. Her paternal grandfather made a lot of money in railroad cars and then founded two schools, the Dayton Academy and the Cooper Female Seminary. He was the first principal of the latter institution. His coregent, her maternal grandfather Pike, also made a fortune, and then built Pike's Opera House for Dayton, apparently because he was very fond of music and wanted to have it available. Natalie's father, Albert Clifford Barney, seems to have reacted in the time-honored way of next generations by forswearing such spiritual interests, for he speedily sold his father's business and devoted himself thereafter to worldly pleasures. But Natalie's mother, Alice Pike, was interested in painting and worked at it. She took lessons from the masters Carolus-Duran and Whistler, becoming in time a respected portrait painter herself. This interest was not permitted to interfere with the social activities she enjoyed. In Washington, as in Paris, Rhode Island, and Maine, the Barneys were forever going to or giving parties.

Natalie Barney, despite her reknown as a salonist with a reputation for intellectual pursuits, never had much of an education. Girls of her time, with her background, simply were not trained to be bluestockings. She and her sister Laura had a French governess, and as children became proficient in French. Then, at the age of ten, she had a year in a French boarding school. She had another year, for what it was worth, at a finishing school in Washington and was then sent abroad for a kind of carefully chaperoned grand tour, visiting Russia and pausing for a time in Germany, where she studied the violin, fencing, and dancing. That was the extent of her schooling. In later life she often astonished friends with her unashamed ignorance of many subjects. On the other hand, she rode a horse excellently, had quantities of pale blonde hair, beautiful if strange pale blue eyes, and a remarkable independence of spirit. Never in all her life did she care what people said about her—and they said a lot.

Natalie's mother, says George Wickes, had a flamboyant personality and in her later years developed a wealthy bohemian style. After her husband's death in 1902 she lived as a merry widow for twenty-nine years, and according to her photographs "grew increasingly youthful and curvaceous." She continued to paint, and developed a fondness for young male models, marrying one who was less than half her age. This marriage did not work out well, but she did not seem unduly embittered, nor did she ever object to Natalie's unconventional sexual tastes even when they became the talk of Paris. The same cannot be said for Albert Clifford Barney, who was scandalized when his elder daughter fell in love with women and paid court to them. He often quarreled with her about it. When Natalie was twenty-two, for example, and the family was spending the year in Paris, she was attracted by a famous courtesan named Liane de Pougy and began sending flowers and amorous letters to the lady, who was amused enough to lead her on. Natalie went to Liane's house in the costume of a page boy, which suited her as she was slender and small; her mother once painted her in such guise. Albert Barney caught his daughter reading a love letter from de Pougy, and was choleric. But Natalie, a child of her time, was a dutiful daughter, within limits. She did not defy him in any open, unseemly manner; she merely continued to go her own way. Indeed, as if to reassure him, she actually got engaged to a man now and then, though the engagements never led to marriage. In one case her fiancé was Lord Alfred Douglas, the notorious lover of Oscar Wilde. Barney may well have thought the threatened scandal of such a son-in-law was worse than anything Natalie might herself bring into the family, and to his relief no more was heard of the projected match.

He never carried his disapproval to extreme lengths. When he died he left his money to both girls equally, so that Laura and Natalie received two and a half million dollars apiece. From then on Natalie made Paris her permanent home. Laura became an enthusiastic supporter of the Bahai religion, but religion of any kind was never an interest of Natalie's. Her first book—a slim volume—came out in 1900, with the title *Quelques portraits-sonnets de femmes.* According to Wickes, it was frankly apprentice work in a conventional nineteenth-century style which she was never, in spite of years of trying, to go beyond. He calls attention to the strange discrepancy between the banality of this style and the daring subject the poems treat, since they are all candidly lesbian. In apparent innocence of this fact, Alice Pike Barney supplied four portraits of women for illustrations.

Barney explained in the preface that she chose to write in French rather than her native English because it was the only language that made her think poetically; writing in French verse seemed to come more naturally to her. Her biographer comments that this fact sums up all the odd aspects of Natalie Barney. Her life was unplanned and casual, like that of the American she was, yet her speech in French was always controlled and precise. No matter how tempestuous her love affairs she remained incurably rational, regarding emotions with detachment and irony. It suited her style best when, a little later, she took to writing and publishing epigrams rather than poems.

Friends of hers at this early stage of her life were Pierre Louÿs, best known in America for his "Songs of Bilitis" and "Aphrodite," and an American-English girl named Pauline Tarn, herself a talented poet who changed her name to Renée Vivien. Louÿs's work influenced Barney's second book, *Five Little Green Dialogues,* published in 1902. Soon after this book appeared, Liane de Pougy broke into print with a scandalous little novel called *A Sapphic Idyll,* which told the story, in barely disguised terms, of Barney's courtship of her. Of Renée Vivien, more hereafter.

The pattern of Barney's life was set. Like all her family she loved to entertain; it was part of their tradition, and she was no exception. In her house and garden poets read their works aloud, musicians played, people danced, and guests, often in costume, strolled about in conversation in a mannerly, stilted style. There were often theatricals—little plays or charades. She had good friends because she was a good friend—"I have sometimes lost friends," she said, "but they have never lost me." Most notable among the men she befriended were Rémy de Gourmont, André Gide, Marcel Schwob, and Paul Valéry. Rémy de Gourmont, who had become a recluse until she sought him out, published a book inspired by her which he called *Letters to an Amazon.* He was really in love with her, and there is no doubt that she was very fond of him.

Her mode of life suited Barney completely. Like Henry James she had coolly made her decision and selected her scene, which did not include the land of her birth. Not that she ever proclaimed her dislike of America, which she sometimes visited; it just was not the place where she lived. Europe was what she wanted and what she found. The half-and-half existence of Edith Wharton, for example, would not have satisfied a woman who wanted to be immersed in France—the French language, French ways of thought. Paradoxically, her way of going about attaining her wishes was peculiarly American in its determination and straightforwardness, and these qualities also characterized Mabel Dodge Luhan.

Mabel was sixteen in 1895, when she left her native Buffalo to attend Miss Graham's Young Ladies' Boarding School in New York. Probably the level of education was much like that of Barney's earliest institution, though she never became particularly fluent in French—or indeed in any foreign language. She learned something of music, dancing, and literature. As a schoolgirl she copied out favorite passages of Shake-speare and the poets in favor at the time, and became a copious diary scribbler. In her memoirs she mentions that she became fond, early in life, of home decorating. At Miss Graham's school she met a girl named Mary Shilleto and was immediately attracted because Mary was out of the ordinary—Mabel, from the earliest time she could remember, was bored with the average. Mary Shilleto was at Miss Graham's school for one chief purpose, to learn English. Though her family came from Cincinnati, she had grown up in Paris with her elder sister Violet; her father represented a large firm there. The Shilleto parents had decided to make the girls attend school in the United States long enough to learn their native language, and to hasten the process they were sent to separate establishments—a brutal but effective treatment. Through Mary, Mabel in time met Violet and was immediately fascinated by this girl, who was interested in poetry, music, philosophy, and religion, subjects on which Mabel had had few discussions in Buffalo. The Shilleto girls persuaded Mabel, who in turn persuaded her mother, to spend the following summer in Europe, to hear Wagner at Bayreuth and go shopping in Paris. Mrs. Ganson needed little persuading, since she had been in Europe before, and even had family connections there. In Paris, reunited with the Shilletos, Mabel noticed that Violet would sometimes slip away from the family apartment and go upstairs to another flat to visit an American girl named Pauline Tarn. Violet explained that these visits had to be clandestine because her father did not approve of Pauline, who insisted on living alone. It was something no girl of their circle was permitted to do, and Mr. Shilleto declared that Pauline was, for this reason, "déclassé,"—evidently one of his favorite words. (Later, when Mabel herself slipped away and had supper unchaperoned with the suitor she was later to marry, though she had already been once married and had a son, Mr. Shilleto declared her also déclassé.) Pauline Tarn was the poet who later rechristened herself. As Renée Vivien, she had a long, troubled affair with Natalie Barney.

Mabel never claimed to be a true Parisian. Like all good architects of his time her second husband, a young Bostonian named Edwin Dodge, preferred the art and architecture of Italy. Mabel's first marriage had been an unadventurous short-lived one with the boy next door. Soon after his death she met Dodge aboard ship to Europe, and not long afterward they married. They bought a villa at Arcetri near Florence, and Edwin set to work remodeling it while Mabel spent happy months and many thousands of dollars doing it up and furnishing it. Exceedingly gregarious all her life, she was never so happy as when she had a houseful of guests, preferably well mixed with stars of the time. Among these notables she entertained Jacques-Emile Blanche—who like many other artists painted her portrait—Gertrude Stein (also a good friend of Natalie Barney), Eleanora Duse, Myrna Loy, and in later years Robert Edmund-Jones and other young men from Harvard. Not having yet found her true forte of writing, Mabel concentrated on collecting furniture, paintings, and people. Like every successful salonist she took a lot of trouble with the food and wine she served, and was also, like most salonists, a catalytic agent, mixing her friends and sampling the results with relish.

When Florence began to bore her she would go to Paris for a change of air. Violet Shilleto died, and Mabel stayed with Mary until that too bored her. She made many friends in Paris and knew her way around the studios as well as the shops, but she never achieved a circle there to rank with that of Natalie Barney. The remarkable Barney, who outlived Mabel and practically everyone else of her time, did not die until she was ninety-five, in 1970, but long before that Mabel had given up Europe and returned to America. In New York she collected another glittering group of friends and became widely known just before World War I for her so-called evenings, at which one might meet anyone at all in the world of art and literature. At that period Mabel fell in love with the young radical John Reed, shed her husband Edwin Dodge, and in due course lost Reed as well. She then married the painter Maurice Sterne, who persuaded her to come out to New Mexico and see the Indians he was painting. Mabel rapidly fell in love with the Southwest and her husband's subjects. It seemed to her that she was intended by fate to help the Indians against an oppressive government, and in the course of this self-selected cause she fell in love with a Taos Indian, Tony Luhan, who, after she got rid of Sterne, became her fourth and last husband. The marriage was most unusual, as few White people had ever entered into such a contract.

Through the years of her long and happy, though odd, life with Tony, Mabel did a lot of helpful things for the Indians in general and Taos in particular. As time went on she began publishing parts of the memoirs she had been writing ever since, if rumor is to be believed, the psychoanalyst Brill advised her to do so. In all she published four volumes of these memoirs and two other books, one about living in Taos and the other about D.H. Lawrence, with whom she had a strange, stormy, quarrelsome relationship, for Lawrence was determined not to be seduced. It was because of Mabel that Lawrence and his wife Frieda, along with their friend Dorothy Brett, came to live permanently, as they thought, in the mountains of New Mexico. Others who stayed under her hospitable roof were Thornton Wilder and his sister Isabel, Robinson Jeffers and his wife, Carl Van Vechten, Leo Stein (Gertrude's brother), and many others. Mabel died in 1962 at the age of eighty-three.

Janet Flanner once told me that she had been part of an exodus of Americans from the Midwest who wanted to get to Paris. Ernest Hemingway was one of these, early in the 1920s, and Flanner knew him well. "It was a time when all of us from the great rolling plains of the midwest wanted to get away from all that space," she explained, "and we went in droves, of course, to Paris." She was born in Indianapolis, where her father founded Flanner House, one of the first American institutions for underprivileged Blacks.

Flanner, who had attended the University of Chicago, wanted to write in surroundings more conducive to work and study than she found in Indianapolis or even Chicago, and in Paris she was happier. In the course of her work there she translated *Claudine à l'école* and *Chéri* by Colette, as well as Georgette Leblanc's *Souvenirs,* memoirs of her life with Maurice Maeterlinck. Flanner also wrote a novel. It was not until four years after she arrived in Paris that, by a happy chance for the new magazine *The New Yorker,* she was asked by Jane Grant, wife of *The New Yorker*'s editor Harold Ross, if she would be willing to write for them a fortnightly letter from Paris. Ross followed up the suggestion with a formal one, and Flanner complied.

Her work in this new genre was inspired. For years, from 1925 to 1965—with the inevitable interruption of the war years—Genêt, to use her nom de plume, sent word to America of all that was going on in Paris and the French press: exhibitions, concerts, gossip, and most important, politics. She carried journalism to the heights of art, and did it all on her own:

> All I really knew about what Ross wished me to write and what I wished for me to write, was that it must be precisely accurate, highly personal, colorful, and ocularly descriptive, and that for sentence style, Gibbon was as good a model as I could bring to mind, he having been the master of antithesis, at once both enriching and economical through his use of opposites. Since my assignment was to tell what the French thought was going on, my only obvious, complete, facile source of information was the French press. At that time, as I remember, there were eight daily secular French newspapers, divergent in political loyalties, and there was as well a theatrical paper called *Comoedia,* which covered every aspect of Parisian entertainment, from the Comédie-Française (including occasional professional notes on the career of Molière) to what was new and nude (in the Folies-Bergères). . . . Paris was still a beautiful, alluring, satisfying city. It was a city of charm and enticement, to foreigners and even to the French themselves. . . . In the early twenties, when I was there, Paris was still yesterday.[2]

What Flanner had been doing all those years was not merely writing a newsletter, but interpreting the whole nation of France to our nation—no small feat, and something nobody else in journalism, other forms of letters or even diplomacy, has ever done. Her style is highly individual, composed of learning leavened by wit, understanding, passion, and compassion. Through her we know the true story of Sylvia Beach and her shabby treatment by James Joyce, something of which Beach herself never complained. With her we live through the anxious days of 1938 and the attempt that was to bring us peace in our time—and failed. In the middle of these frightening moments it is amusing and relieving to read of French reaction to the Darryl Zanuck film *Suez,* in which de Lesseps is pictured as being in love with Empress Eugénie. They naturally took a poor view of it, and in London a reviewer wrote: "What would Americans think of a British film of old Kentucky, with Lincoln as a plantation owner courting Harriet Beecher Stowe to the theme song of Alexander's Ragtime Band?" To which Flanner remarked blithely: "Lots of Americans would probably think it was grand."

She wrote about the Spanish Civil War and the refugees who thronged Perpignan. We hear of the rise of Picasso, Hitler's conquest of Poland, and incidentally, the murder of an American girl tourist. There is a sudden burst of social gaiety in the capital city, and then suddenly all is over. At the end of *Paris Was Yesterday* Flanner signed off with an article entitled "War in Our Time."

In 1944 she returned and took up once again the reins of her work. In *Paris Journal, 1944-1965* her readers were given more of the same mixture, which now included a close and fascinating study of de Gaulle in what amounts to an almost day-by-day account of the development of this extraordinary man. Interspersed with such matters as the price of black truffles, French opinion of Adlai Stevenson (enthusiastically favorable), and the death of Braque, it gives as no other form the flavor of the country and city. The French are difficult to understand, but if such a thing is at all possible, it is thanks to Janet Flanner.

NOTES

1. George Wickes, *The Amazon of Letters: The Life and Loves of Natalie Barney* (New York: Putnam, 1976).
2. Janet Flanner, *Paris Was Yesterday, 1925-1939* (New York: Viking Press, 1972), pp. xx-xxi.

8.

Publishing in Paris

Hugh D. Ford

Some years ago a longtime male resident of Paris observed that one of the remarkable facts about Montparnasse between wars was that its organizers and leaders were mostly women. He contended that they had shaped, directed, and nourished the social, artistic, and literary life of that ceaselessly fascinating cosmopolitan cultural quarter that once flourished on the Left Bank of the Seine. His observation finds an absorbing and exciting documentation in the accomplishments of a group of women editors and publishers who for a few years in the twenties and thirties made literary midwifery a career.

Their story rightly begins in 1921, when Florence Gilliam, an American, founded the first English-language magazine of the arts on the Continent. She named it *Gargoyle*. The story continues with the celebrated publication, in 1922, of *Ulysses;* with the arrival in Paris, two years later, of the *Little Review;* and with the opening, in 1925, of *This Quarter,* a magazine supported and coedited by a Scot named Ethel Moorhead. That same year the Crosbys released the first Black Sun volume, a collection of Caresse's poems to Harry. In 1926, Helena Rubinstein sequestered herself on the Right Bank and shuttled funds across the river and into her husband's Black Manikin Press, thus proving again that what the Left often needed the Right could often supply. The following year, Maria Jolas as patron and coeditor brought forth the first number of *transition,* the most aggressively revolutionary of the small magazines. In 1928, to the amazement of all, Nancy Cunard opened the Hours Press, and by 1929 Sylvia Beach had issued two more books by James Joyce. In 1930, Barbara Harrison formed her own publishing company; and in 1931, Gertrude Stein and Alice Toklas did the same, reckoning the time had come to publish the works of Gertrude Stein (or in plain English, "to shove the unshoveable"). They sold a Picasso and opened their own firm. Stein called it Plain Editions.

From this galaxy I have plucked six luminaries whose glorious achievements helped make Paris an Anglo-American third world of the arts for two decades. Some might say I am starting with the brightest: Sylvia Beach, the first American publisher in postwar France. Hers was a monumental task she might never have assumed had the moral climate here and in England been then what it is today. This clergyman's daughter from Princeton had set out to publish *Ulysses*. Even *she* thought Joyce was rash to entrust his book to such a funny little publisher. A year after she began, in February 1922, a Dijon printer delivered the first copies. Despite disputes, misunderstandings, and delays, publisher and author survived the ordeal, and Sylvia's part in the triumph, which linked her name forever with the author's, was widely acclaimed. On reflection, Sylvia concluded that while accommodating a genius did have its rewards, it could also be a grindingly exasperating experience. It was five percent accident and ninety-five percent hard toil. It was the result of an amazing capacity for sheer donkey work, for doing, frequently alone, the fatiguing and monotonous tasks ordinarily done by the anonymous many. Though Sylvia Beach was not creative, she had what every publisher needs: intuition. She knew she was going to play a vital part in the "birthing" of a great work. For the next decade, while she presided over the many editions of *Ulysses,* she never thought of herself as anything more than a fortunate novice. She rejected the entreaties of Frank Harris and D.H. Lawrence to publish their persecuted books, patiently explaining that one was enough. Around her (in the shop) writers and publishers congregated. To them she was an inspiration. If she, who knew nothing about printing books, had successfully brought forth, in a foreign country, a 732-page novel, why could not others, with more modest aims, do as well? But if they tried, they discovered that she was inimitable—and very astute. She accepted one author, never wrote anything of her own, read Joyce's galleys with devotion, supervised the printing, and then distributed the book herself. She is what she has been called: the most famous and successful amateur publisher of this century.

While Florence Gilliam's *Gargoyle* struggled to celebrate its first birthday, other little magazines in Paris like *transition* and *This Quarter* survived the strains of puberty and at least advanced into middle age before expiring. The memorable exception was the *Little Review,* which after a decade and a half of vigorous life, died a painless death because its editors concluded that contributors no longer knew what they were doing. The publication in serial form of a substantial portion of *Ulysses* is the *Little Review*'s single greatest achievement. Although it is their shared masterpiece, Margaret Anderson and Jane Heap must be credited, singly and together, with lots more, though this means acknowledging the enriching influence of Ezra Pound on the magazine from 1916 to 1919. From England, he wrote the editors telling them of Eliot, Joyce, Wyndham Lewis, Ford, and Yeats. In May 1917 Anderson appointed him foreign editor, thus ensuring him a place where he and the others could appear regularly. With Pound's infusion the *Little Review* grew from a dull and rather pretentious publication into a formidable dispenser of modernism. Pound was as delighted as the editors with the transformation, but Anderson always stoutly denied that she and Heap were unduly influenced by their man in London. Pound had sent *Ulysses,* but he had not influenced her to publish it. She did that because she had loved *A Portrait of the Artist As a Young Man,* and because the opening chapter of *Ulysses* contained such "magic words."

When someone asked Anderson what critical standards guided her editorial decisions, hinting that maybe there were none, she replied: *"Mon dieu,* did I have any standards? I had nothing *but!"* Anderson could be ornery; she could be an imperious arbiter of taste; her self-assurance could escalate to inflexibility. She continued: "I would accept only that writing which met, even in the slightest degree, my touchstone judgments." A touchstone to her was the "kind of person who could prove that, in his case, the despised terms 'I like' or 'I don't like' were important, authentic, and *right."* The morning *Ulysses* arrived, Anderson had been brought to the verge of tears when, rushing through the opening chapter, she had read: "Ineluctible modality of the visible." Heap shared Anderson's emotion, and they determined to publish it at once. "We were terribly moved; we kept saying, 'What ART!'" To a reader puzzled by Joyce's meaning, Margaret explained: "I don't think of what it means . . . Joyce has produced a paragraph of great prose—in other words, ART."[1] Anderson the touchstone was inviolable.

In 1919 Pound resigned. The next year came the celebrated "obscenity" trial of Joyce's book, which despite a spirited defense by John Quinn, the author's friend and patron, ended in glorious defeat. Art never claimed two more regal and pugnacious martyrs than the editors of the *Little Review.* Following the trial the magazine became a quarterly and then appeared irregularly. The contents were often unpredictable, at times uneven, and the celebrities of the decade—Stein, Cocteau, Cummings, Hemingway, and Picabia (who occasionally doubled as advisor)—were often joined by the conspicuously ungifted. Anderson's interest in the magazine waned too, and Heap assumed increasing responsibilities. By 1924, with the *Little Review* temporarily berthed in Paris, she was virtually in command and remained so to the end.

Jane Heap came to the *Little Review* during the Chicago period (1914-1917). A deep and orderly thinker, a skillful but sluggish writer, a pertinacious critic, and a born editor, Jane Heap provided intellectual ballast and emotional balance. She was a brilliant talker. It was she who distilled their opinions on art and gave the *Little Review* a quotable working formula: "To express the emotions of life is to live. To express the life of the emotions is to make art." Aphoristic proclamations like these released from Anderson floods of superlatives: "To me the expression, the formulation, of Jane's thoughts amounted to genius." Anderson herself had no pretensions of knowing the things about life and art that Jane knew and articulated; so she cast herself as an appreciator and demander, hounding her friend, whom she called the creator, to convert her nimble, piercing, and intelligent talk into writing, and hence into the permanent record of the *Little Review*. Her entreaties effective, Heap once commented: "You pushed me into the arena, and I performed to keep you quiet." [2]

In 1929 at the last rites, the editors explained why after fifteen years they had joined to inter the *Little Review*. Anderson first: "I can no longer go on publishing a magazine in which no one really knows what he is talking about." [3] Heap followed: "For years, we offered the *Little Review* as a trial-track for racers. We hoped to find artists who could run with the great artists of the past . . . who could make new records. But you can't get race horses from mules. We have given space . . . to 23 new systems of art (all now dead), representing 19 countries. In all of this we have not brought forward anything approaching a masterpiece except *Ulysses*." [4] Even a despondent Heap could not dim the *Little Review*'s imposing reputation as the place where so much of our enduring art originally appeared. For this we are indebted to Anderson the founder, appreciator, and demander, who, just fourteen years ago, reexpressed her indebtedness to Heap, the creator, this way: "If I could start a new *Little Review* today, I would be satisfied if I had only one contributor: Jane Heap." [5]

Nancy Cunard offers stunning proof (if any be needed) that publishers can sometimes be at least as engrossing as the writers they publish. Cunard was as much an amateur as Sylvia Beach, but she was an amateur with wealth (a handy convenience for anyone planning to publish books), and although she did not quite exhaust her portion of the Cunard fortune practicing her avocation, she nonetheless spent lavishly almost to the end, when she suddenly and uncharacteristically turned parsimonious. No Joyce inspired Cunard, but she did have Louis Aragon and the company of a circle of surrealists as well as the support and encouragement of accommodating old friends like George Moore and Norman Douglas.

Monumental incredulity greeted her announcement in 1928 that she would not only open a press but print books by hand. It seemed inconceivable that this highborn renegade socialite and gifted poet, whose name in the twenties had been linked with Wyndham Lewis, Aldous Huxley, and other British and American writers and artists—and now Aragon—could really be serious. For one thing, where would she ever find the time? While Montparnassians waited, dubious, Cunard sought the guidance of two fledgling printers, Virginia and Leonard Woolf, who, while not intentionally dissuasive, let go with an anguished warning that she promptly forgot: "My dear," they chorused, "your hands will always be covered with ink!" [6] Others echoed the Woolfs' cry, but just as ineffectually, for Cunard, once determined, always pursued her own path.

Cunard's is probably the only press that can claim the distinction of having been born in a stable. It was one of the outbuildings that came with a Norman farmhouse (an hour's drive from Paris) she purchased in 1927, so that she could live, love, and print books in privacy. The press she christened the Hours, a name at once dullish, but suitable, and appropriately suggestive of work. In place of stanchions, she installed an immense Mathieu press, at least a century old, on which her friend Bill Bird had only recently hand-printed Hemingway's *In Our Time* and books by Williams, Ford, and Pound. Bird also supplied an experienced instructor who years earlier had worked as a printer's devil, and who, to his alarm, soon found this amateur annoyingly unimpressionable and as unconventional as the books she intended to publish. Efforts to instruct his charge, as well as Aragon, in the intricacies of the Black Art failed dismally. Cunard and Aragon took a conspiratorial delight in ignoring his precepts. She would learn from him, she announced quickly, all she possibly could; meanwhile she would put innovation and experimentation ahead of his time-worn practices. No one, Cunard thought later, ever launched out on a new endeavor so sail-less, mast-less, provision-less, uncompassed, and abashed. Miraculously, after a year, she had realized a few of her goals. Of the announced volumes of modern poetry those by Iris Tree and Pound had not appeared, but others by Alvaro Guevara and Aragon had. So had the prose pieces of Norman

Douglas, Richard Aldington, and George Moore. The total reached eight volumes, all hand-printed. Cunard attributed her success to hard work, a few celebrated authors, almost total ignorance of the customs and practices of printing, and good luck.

Of the twenty-four Hours books Cunard published, sixteen lay ahead at the start of 1930. They would consist of collections of poetry by Roy Campbell, Laura Riding, Walter Lowenfels, Ezra Pound, and Robert Graves; a catalogue for an exhibit of paintings by the American Eugene MacCown; prose by Aldington, Havelock Ellis, and George Moore; and two books which would become memorials to her inspiration and ingenuity. One—titled *Henry-Music*—was a mosaic of the arts combining poetry, impeccable printing, photomontage, and music—all in one volume. The other might be called a literary discovery.

In 1930 Cunard exchanged the bucolic pleasures of the Norman countryside for the bibulous excitement of Paris. From her new location in rue Guenegaud, near the river, she announced the Hours Press would hold a poetry contest. A prize of ten pounds would be paid to the author of the best poem on the subject of time. The notice released an avalanche of verse. In a few weeks over a hundred specimens had descended on the Hours Press shop, ranging from doggerel to a kind of sham metaphysics. From the accumulation Cunard and Richard Aldington (her co-judge) sifted out the entries that might charitably qualify for the award, and then stoically resigned themselves to giving the prize to the best of the mediocre entries, unless by some miracle a first-rate poem turned up before closing time. None did. The deadline arrived and passed. Unbeknownst to them, a winning poem was in the making, and it was Cunard who discovered it the morning after the contest closed when, on opening the shop, she spied tucked beneath the door a small folder bearing the strange word *Whoroscope,* under which was a signature: Samuel Beckett. The name meant nothing to either, but the poem inside filled them with admiration. "What remarkable lines, what images and analogies, what vivid coloring; indeed, what technique." [7] Beckett was summoned and told that he had won the competition. In turn, he told the astonished judges that he had only learned of the contest the previous day and had composed the entire poem of ninety-eight lines in two frenzied stints separated by a refreshing interlude at the Cochon de Lait for a guzzle of salad and Chambertin, after which, near dawn, he had delivered it to her door. *Whoroscope,* suited in red covers and adorned with a white sash that bore the proud notice it was the prize-winner, soon appeared, prominently placed, in Cunard's display window. It was the author's first separately published work.

Publishing in Paris was financially profitless. Except for Sylvia Beach and one or two others, most publishers invested far more in their endeavors than they ever took in. For the few whose presses rested securely on a foundation of wealth, there was no need to worry about showing a return. With ample funds, time, and access to fine materials and the services of gifted draughtsmen, they were in the enviable position of being able to produce books which, even measured by the demanding standards of most small presses, would have to be considered sumptuous. That, to our lasting benefit, is exactly what they did.

Barbara Harrison and Caresse Crosby (whose names have probably never before been joined) shared the refined connoisseur's appreciation of the visual appearance of the books they published. The result was that the thirteen publications of Barbara Harrison's press (organized in 1930 with Glenway Wescott and Monroe Wheeler) set standards of design and typography that no other little press exceeded or even matched. Her books (most of them sleeved in slipcases) were printed on exotic papers, like Madagascar or Imperial Japan vellum or handmade Auvergne; the last, a pure rag paper ("as soft as old handkerchiefs"), was used in the Harrison edition of Aesop's *Fables,* which came suited in blue covers made from discarded aprons worn for years by the schoolchildren of the Auvergne region. Alexander Calder illustrated the *Fables* with linear drawings that still vibrate with subtle ironic interpretations. As carefully chosen were type faces: a large 11-point Bodoni type, for example, admirably set off a volume of Bret Harte's tales that the directors hoped would spur a resurgence of interest in the "good and handsome Californian" whose books, they complained, had often suffered by being printed on "muddy-looking" paper. The Harrison of Paris press combined the classics and the moderns (Thomas Mann, Katherine Anne Porter, Glenway Wescott); it continued the tradition of expert bookmaking exemplified by the work of William Morris and Robert Gibbings. Its legacy is a priceless and inspiring inheritance.

While Barbara Harrison benefited from the expertise of her associates, Caresse and Harry Crosby had almost no knowledge of bookmaking and publishing, and at the start depended for direction on an obscure Parisian printer whose jobs prior to the Crosbys' sudden appearance consisted mainly of wedding invitations. He 'viewed the two Americans as eccentrics and their order for lavishly printed volumes of their poetry as an extravagance that would pass as suddenly as it had materialized. Their Black Sun Press outlived (eight years in Paris) and published more books than any of its competitors; and except for two D.H. Lawrence stories, Caresse guided to completion the best of them. The year Harry died, 1929, Black Sun issued fifteen books, including

works by Kay Boyle, Joyce, MacLeish, and Jolas, as well as the customary selection by the publishers. In their partnership Harry usually decided which authors and books would be published and Caresse
functioned as a general factotum and trouble-shooter. When Picasso
refused to provide a portrait of Joyce for the Black Sun edition of *Work
in Progress,* Caresse told him he would regret his decision, and immediately signed up Brancusi, who within hours produced a quintessential
portrait of the author. Caresse coaxed from an ailing and tormented
Hart Crane his long-delayed poem, *The Bridge.* Harry provided Crane
with the material comforts he did or did not need, and Caresse con-
ducted the poem-producing correspondence with the poet and supervised the first publication of *The Bridge* in Paris in 1930. In the same
year, Caresse, now being advised by Ezra Pound, whose *Imaginary
Letters* was one of her first books, and by close friends Kay Boyle and
Jacques Porel, made a decision that would briefly transform the Black
Sun from a small press specializing in limited editions into a commercial firm competing with the prosperous Tauchnitz Company, publishers
of paperback reprints of English classics and a few moderns. Could one
launch an English-language paperback series limited to contemporary
American and French authors, and do as well, or better?

Convinced one could, Caresse announced the formation of Crosby
Continental Editions, and under that imprint in 1932, she issued ten
inexpensive paperback reprints beginning with *The Torrents of Spring.*
After six months sales were dismal, and Caresse, eying America as a
possible market, journeyed to New York in hopes of selling the series to
the highest bidder. Bennett Cerf said no; Dick Simon said no: Americans would not buy paperbacks, no matter how cheap. Her protests
notwithstanding, they remained immovable; and their firmness brought
an abrupt end to Continental Editions and a temporary eclipse of the
Black Sun. When it shone again three years later (1936) and then off
and on for another decade, sometimes in Europe and sometimes in
America, its imprint was once more affixed to limited editions as daz-
zling as those early bright Paris creations.

For almost two decades this band of intrepid amateur publishers, for
reasons as diverse and complicated as the people themselves, stocked
our culture with artfully made books of substantial worth. Jointly they
turned Montparnasse into a busy, exuberant, and innovative nonprofit
publishing center. By providing outlets for all who had things to say,
they fostered creative productiveness. They heartened those whose
books had been banned in their own countries, and those whose literary
experiments had been rejected by cautious, sales-minded publishers.
Against the established book producers—overcommercialized, undercul-

turalized, timid—they formed a fearless, ready, and sure bulwark. They cultivated an intimacy with their authors that commercial houses, then as well as now, almost always lacked. With both jointly involved in preparing a book for publication, theirs was a mutually creative and stimulating collaboration. Their industry and productivity helped repudiate the fatuous image of Montparnasse. Because of what they did it became more difficult to dismiss it as a place where expatriates languished and frittered away their time and talent. Their existence symbolized dedication, determination, protest. Theirs was an aesthetic flowering and rebellion, the reverberations of which we continue to feel.

NOTES

1. Margaret Anderson to Solita Solano, 28 August 1967. Unpublished letter.
2. Ibid.
3. Margaret Anderson, "Editorial," *Little Review* (May 1929): 3.
4. Jane Heap, "Lost: A Renaissance," *Little Review* (May 1929): 5.
5. Margaret Anderson to Solita Solano, 28 August 1967. Unpublished letter.
6. Nancy Cunard, *These Were the Hours* (Carbondale: Southern Illinois University Press, 1969), p. 8.
7. Ibid., p. 111.

9.

Poets and Versifiers, Singers and Signifiers: Women of the Harlem Renaissance

Cheryl A. Wall

In the words of Langston Hughes, the 1920s were a time "when the Negro was in vogue." [1] Culturally, the Black presence was more visible than it had ever been before; so much so that Black artists proclaimed a renaissance. Every Broadway season during 1921-29 saw the opening of a new Black production. White Americans listened to Black music or an imitation thereof, and liked it so well they dubbed the 1920s the Jazz Age. Publishers responded to a growing demand for literature about Blacks. For the first time, Black authors were actively courted by major publishing concerns; men like Hughes, Countee Cullen, and Claude McKay all reached relatively large audiences. Politically, W.E.B. DuBois and the NAACP, Charles Johnson and the Urban League, and in the most dramatic way, Marcus Garvey and the United Negro Improvement Association were voicing newly militant demands. The pages of the most influential journals of the day—*The Crisis, Opportunity, Negro World,* and *The Messenger*—were often devoted to discussion of long-standing social problems and progressive solutions advanced by the so-called New Negro. Intellectuals like Alain Locke, James Weldon Johnson, DuBois, and others saw art as a key weapon in the New Negro's struggle. Discussing what he considered the Negro's racial gifts,

Locke wrote: "The especially cultural recognition they win should in turn prove the key to that revaluation of the Negro which must precede or accompany any considerable further betterment of race relationships."[2] Each play, poem, and novel was closely examined to determine its role in the fight. Old myths were being destroyed, and the images that would replace them had to be chosen with great care.

This exciting atmosphere stirred the interest of Black women as well as Black men. To a degree even greater than Black male writers, Black women had few models. Although Phillis Wheatley had been the heroine of the first chapter of Afro-American literary history, few nineteenth-century Black women had followed her lead. Of those who had, most printed their poems and novels privately. Only Frances Watkins Harper, an abolitionist and feminist as well as poet and novelist, achieved comparatively widespread recognition. Proportionately few slave narratives, the most important genre of nineteenth-century Afro-American literature, were written by women. By contrast, the most prolific novelist of the Harlem Renaissance was Jessie Fauset, whose four books were published over a ten-year period. Nella Larsen's novels were frequently reviewed and praised. For Zora Neale Hurston, the twenties were years of apprenticeship. Today her work is being rediscovered and acclaimed and she is being accorded her rightful place as a major writer of the period. The Harlem Renaissance was certainly not a male phenomenon.

As in other cultural awakenings, the renaissance produced more versifiers than poets, and a large number of these were women. No woman rivaled the achievement of Langston Hughes or Countee Cullen. Only in music did women and men share equal billing; Bessie Smith's reputation is as lustrous as that of any artist of the period. The twenties marked the heyday of classic blues singers, all of whom were female. Free of the burdens of an alien tradition, a Bessie Smith could establish the standard of her art; in the process she would compose a more honest poetry than any of her literary sisters'. They lacked the connection to those cultural traditions which shaped Smith's art; nonetheless, some produced work which "signified." The work of the greatest signifier, Zora Neale Hurston, was born, like Bessie's, from folk tradition and on occasion even from performance.

Nathan Huggins has described the debilitating effect on their art of Black writers' self-consciousness; this affected no group as severely as the female poets of the Harlem Renaissance.[3] Their poems reflect far less of the race consciousness characteristic of their male counterparts. To understand their poems it is necessary to understand more about the context in which they were written. Black women were doubly oppressed, as Blacks and as women, and they were highly aware of the degrading stereotypes commonly applied to them. Some idea of the mood of the New Negro woman may be drawn from an essay by Elise Johnson McDougald who wrote:

> She [the Negro woman] is conscious that what is left of chivalry is not directed toward her. She realizes that the ideals of beauty, built up in the fine arts, have excluded her almost entirely. Instead, the grotesque Aunt Jemimas of the street-car advertisements, proclaim only an ability to serve without grace or loveliness. Nor does the drama catch her finest spirit. She is most often used to provoke the mirthless laugh of ridicule; or to portray feminine viciousness or vulgarity not peculiar to Negroes. This is the shadow over her.[4]

This speaks to the negative images that defined Black women as mammies, mulattoes, and whores. The whore image was most vicious because it was the most difficult to defend oneself against; its victims conformed to no easily distinguishable physical type. It was fairly easy to know who was not a mulatto even if it was difficult to say for sure who was. In a society reluctant to recognize sexuality in most women, Black women were burdened with an almost exclusively sexual identity. Part of the conservatism found in the writings of the poets of the period reflects a determination not to conform in even the slightest manner to the hateful stereotypes. Certain subjects, particularly sex, were taboo, and the language was mostly genteel.

The best known poet of the period, Georgia Douglas Johnson, was born in 1886 in Atlanta, a self-described "little yellow girl." After graduating from Atlanta University, she continued her education at the Oberlin Conservatory. Johnson soon gave up her early ambition to become a composer. She had been working as a schoolteacher when President Taft appointed her husband recorder of deeds in Washington, D.C.; for years this post was the chief patronage plum offered the nation's Black politicians. The Johnson home was a favorite meetingplace for young writers; Zora Neale Hurston was among those who participated in the literary discussions held there. Johnson's relatively high social status and educational accomplishment were typical of Black women writers of the day.[5]

Johnson was the most conventional and popular of the women poets. Her supporters included the most respected literary men of her generation: William Stanley Braithwaite, W.E.B. DuBois, and Alain Locke wrote the introductions to her three volumes of poems. Perhaps, as the author of "I Want to Die While You Love Me," hers was considered the true voice of femininity. In any case, this became her most frequently anthologized poem:

> I want to die while you love me,
> While yet you hold me fair,
> While laughter lies upon my lips
> And lights are in my hair.
>
> I want to die while you love me,
> I could not bear to see,
> The glory of this perfect day,
> Grow dim—or cease to be.
>
> I want to die while you love me.
> Oh! who would care to live
> Till love has nothing more to ask,
> And nothing more to give?
>
> I want to die while you love me,
> And bear to that still bed
> Your kisses, turbulent, unspent,
> To warm me when I'm dead.[6]

This regular meter and rhyme are characteristic of Johnson's work, as are the inverted syntax and poetic diction. Love is her favorite subject, rivaled somewhat by religion, and always treated sentimentally. While her poems are all derivative in the extreme, it is not difficult to see why they won her a popular following.

Some of the pressures operating in the lives of the women poets are illustrated by the fact that Johnson's first book of poems, *The Heart of a Woman*, published in 1918, contained no poems about Black life. Johnson's explanation for this, and evidently she felt compelled to proffer one, was that she wished to attract attention to her work using "universal" themes before she presented any poems with racial subject matter. Even in her second book, *Bronze*, racial references are oblique. Like Countee Cullen, Johnson feared the consequences of being labelled "a Negro poet." It is fully understandable that she would hesitate to experiment with language or theme, or in any way reject a tradition that had not yet admitted any Black woman—or man, for that matter. Her compromise necessarily yielded inferior verse.

A less popular but far more interesting poet was Anne Spencer (1882-1975), who began publishing during the renaissance years although she had long written poems for her private pleasure. Spencer was encouraged in her efforts by James Weldon Johnson, then field secretary of the NAACP and himself an important poet. At Johnson's suggestion, many Black writers began to make stopovers in Lynchburg, Virginia, Spencer's home, during their travels South; thus Spencer was kept abreast of ideas and trends in the New Negro movement. Johnson also arranged for the publication of Spencer's poems. Beginning with his seminal anthology, *The Book of American Negro Poetry,* which appeared in 1922, Spencer's poems became a staple of almost every major anthology of Black American poetry published through the 1950s. Still her poems were not collected into a volume until 1977.[7]

Spencer used the traditions of English poetry, but she was not a conventional poet. Her best poems remain fresh and strikingly original. One of these, "At the Carnival," offers a finely hued, evocative description of a tawdry street fair. Onlookers like "the limousine lady" and "the bull-necked man," "the unholy incense" of the sausage and garlic booth, the dancing tent where "a quivering female-thing gestured assignations," and the crooked games of chance combine to produce an atmosphere of unrelieved ugliness and depravity. Yet the possibility of beauty exists even here, in the person of a young female diver, the "Naiad of the Carnival Tank." Her presence transforms the scene. Usually Spencer's references to reality are much more indirect; she rarely used racial themes in her poetry. An autobiographical statement she composed for Countee Cullen's anthology, *Caroling Dusk,* suggests the reason: "I write about the things I love. But have not civilized articulation for the things I hate. I proudly love being a Negro woman— it's so involved and interesting. *We* are the PROBLEM—the great national game of TABOO." [8] Spencer's words reveal a tension that she never reconciled, aesthetically at least, and her poems contain few clues to their author's racial identity. But Spencer's poems evince a richness of imagery and verbal wit that render the epithet "lady poet" as wholly inappropriate for her as it is inevitable for Georgia Douglas Johnson.

Johnson and Spencer were considerably older than the best known New Negro poets, and neither lived in Harlem, which set the tone for so much of the literature. Perhaps as a result, their poetry is far from characteristic of the period as a whole. Younger women, like Gwendolyn Bennett and Helene Johnson, reveal a more typical race consciousness and a stronger empathy with the rhythms of Black urban life. In "To a Dark Girl" Gwendolyn Bennett projects positive images of Black womanhood:

> *I love you for your brownness*
> *And rounded darkness of your breast.*
> *I love you for the breaking sadness in your voice*
> *And shadows where your wayward eye-lids rest.*

Something of old forgotten queens
Lurks in the lithe abandon of your walk
And something of the shackled slave
Sobs in the rhythm of your talk.

Oh, little brown girl, born for sorrows mate
Keep all you have of queenliness,
Forgetting that you once were slave,
And let your full lips laugh at Fate! [9]

Bennett's speaker echoes central themes of the period: the celebration of Blackness and the affirmation of an African heritage. But in choosing to make only vague references to the historical past, in relying on the simplistic contrast between queen and slave, she fails to make a memorable poetic statement even as she reinforces a necessary political one. Even when exploring racial themes Bennett chose not to employ characteristically Black language. Compare her poem to Nikki Giovanni's wildly inventive "Ego Tripping" which is also a tribute to Black women set in a historical context, but which is the work of a poet secure enough to experiment with language as boldly as she can.

The one female poet of the Harlem Renaissance who was inspired by the speech patterns of the newly urbanized migrants was Helene Johnson, whose "Poem" is immediately identifiable as belonging to the era.

Little brown boy,
Slim, dark, big-eyed,
Crooning songs to your banjo
Down at the Lafayette—
Gee, boy, I love the way you hold your head,
High sort of and a bit to one side,
Like a prince, a jazz prince. And I love
Your eyes flashing, and your hands,
And your patent-leathered feet,
And your shoulders jerking the jig-wa.
And I love your teeth flashing,
And the way your hair shines in the spotlight
Like it was the real stuff.
Gee, brown boy, I loves you all over.
I'm glad I'm a jig. I'm glad I can
Understand your dancin' and your
Singin', and feel all the happiness
And joy and don't care in you.
Gee, boy, when you sing, I can close my ears
And hear tom toms just as plain.
Listen to me, will you, what do I know
About tom toms? But I like the word, sort of,
Don't you? It belongs to us.
Gee, boy, I love the way you hold your head,

And the way you sing, and dance,
And everything.
Say, I think you're wonderful. You're
Allright with me,
You are.[10]

This is an exuberant celebration of Black culture during the 1920s. Johnson's use of free verse and Harlem slang liberate her poem. The Lafayette Theater was a Harlem landmark and it featured vaudeville entertainment by and for Blacks; its productions were both like and unlike the string of Broadway successes initiated by the legendary "Shuffle Along." The audience here had a proprietary interest in the entertainment. In depicting a banjo-playing "jazz prince," Johnson deftly suggests the legacy of slavery and its positive impact on a freer, more assertive period. She reclaims the banjo as a racial symbol, discarding its stereotypically servile associations. Likewise, she makes the singing, dancing Black man a positive figure, rather than the object of ridicule and condescension. Her speaker's self-consciousness about the word *tom toms* indicates Johnson's sensitivity to the dangers of exotic primitivism. This poet was not swept away by the atavistic currents of the time; her vision is securely rooted in urban reality.

Gwendolyn Bennett and Helene Johnson were rather late arrivals on the Harlem scene. Bennett's loyalties were divided between poetry and painting, and Helene Johnson was so young that she was scarcely taken seriously. Both published relatively few poems. Better known and more typical of the women of the period was the poetry of Jessie Fauset.

The most prolific Black novelist of the day as well as a poet, Jessie Fauset (1882-1961) could fairly be called the archetypal New Negro woman. The daughter of an old and very distinguished Philadelphia family, Jessie had enjoyed a stable and happy childhood. Her father, the Reverend Redmon Fauset, a minister in the African Methodist Episcopal Church, had been born a free Black in 1833. To his daughter, he cut a noble figure as he ministered to small bands of worshippers in New Jersey backwaters, as well as to the more substantial congregations of Philadelphia's Negro community. Anna and Redmon Fauset not only gave their children a strong moral example, but a measure of security out of the reach of most Black parents of their day.[11] In part as a consequence of her family's economic and social status, Jessie Fauset was able to acquire an education exceptional for any woman of her generation. After becoming the first Black woman to earn a degree from Cornell University, where she was elected to Phi Beta Kappa, she continued her studies at the University of Pennsylvania and the Sorbonne. For several years Fauset taught high school French in Washington, D.C., where she came into contact with that city's Black elite. Among the distinguished people she met during this period was W.E.B. DuBois, for whom she had the greatest respect and admiration. Herself firmly committed to racial uplift, Fauset began to contribute articles and reviews to *The Crisis* as early as 1912. Several years later, having moved to Harlem—which as Langston Hughes observed "was like a magnet for the Negro intellectual, pulling him from everywhere"—Fauset became literary editor of *The Crisis*.[12]

In her position, Fauset's willingness to grow, intellectually and politically, was impressive. She contributed articles on a wide variety of subjects, using each issue of the magazine to enlarge her personal perspective on the world. On occasion, she wrote on educational themes and regularly reported activities of Black women's groups. Often she chose topics intended to illustrate the validity of DuBois's philosophy of Pan-Africanism: biographical sketches of Black heroes in other societies, translations and reviews of literature from Africa and the Caribbean, and accounts of significant meetings devoted to the Pan-African cause. Her extensive travels furthered the development of her internationalist viewpoint, and she shared reports of her travels with *Crisis* readers. She visited the countries of what is now called the Third World as well as European capitals. Although Fauset made three extended trips to Paris during the 1920s, like most other Black American travelers she had no contact with the expatriate community there.

Through her work on *The Crisis* and her personal acquaintance with writers of the Harlem Renaissance, Jessie Fauset emerged as an important figure in the Harlem literary community. Although it could pay very little, *The Crisis* was a major showcase for Black writers; among its other functions, it allowed them to become well known enough to attract the interest of White editors and publishers. As literary editor, Fauset decided what poetry and fiction would appear. Her literary tastes were far less conservative than those of DuBois, and she saw to it that *The Crisis* reflected a broad spectrum of the Black literature of the day. For example, it was Jessie Fauset who first received and read "The Negro Speaks of Rivers" in 1921. After showing the poem to DuBois, she wrote to Langston Hughes and thereby initiated a relationship that was to last throughout the decade. Years later, Hughes asserted that "Jessie Fauset at the *Crisis*, Charles Johnson at *Opportunity*, and Alain Locke in Washington, were the three people who midwifed the so-called New Negro literature into being. Kind and critical—but not too critical for the young—they nursed us along until our books were born."[13] Fauset took an active interest in the careers of young authors, lending advice and encouragement, and, like Georgia Douglas Johnson, opening her home as a salon where writers could share ideas and fellowship. Her solicitude was appreciated. In his memoir *A Long Way from Home*, McKay wrote of Fauset: "All the radicals liked her, although in her social viewpoint she was away over on the other side of the fence." [14]

Unfortunately Fauset's own writing lacks the creative spark she admired and nurtured in others. The subject of most of her poems is love and the tone is usually ironic. It is not irony like that found in the blues however. The personae of Fauset's *vers de société* sound more like the worldly wise lady of T.S. Eliot's "Portrait." Fauset's penchant for French titles strengthens this effect and places the poetry in what amounts to cultural limbo. Consider "La Vie C'est la Vie," her most often anthologized poem:

> *On summer afternoons I sit*
> *Quiescent by you in the park,*
> *And idly watch the sunbeams gild*
> *And tint the ash-trees' bark.*
>
> *Or else I watch the squirrels frisk*
> *And chaffer in the grassy lane;*
> *And all the while I mark your voice*
> *Breaking with love and pain.*
>
> *I know a woman who would give*
> *Her chance of heaven to take my place;*
> *To see the love-light in your eyes,*
> *The love-glow on your face!*
>
> *And there's a man whose lightest word*
> *Can set my chilly blood afire;*
> *Fulfillment of his least behest*
> *Defines my life's desire.*
>
> *But he will none of me, nor I*
> *Of you. Nor you of her. 'Tis said*
> *The world is full of jests like these,—*
> *I wish that I were dead.* [15]

This poem moves carefully from the serenity of the first stanza to the agony and frustration of the last. On first reading, the concluding line is indeed shocking and affecting; the poem's sentiments have obvious popular appeal. But "La Vie C'est la Vie" has serious flaws. The first two stanzas need to move slowly if the contrast between external calm and inner turmoil is to be made clear, but each line should advance the poem's meaning. "Or else I watch the squirrels frisk/And chaffer in the grassy lane" adds little. The language shifts uneasily from the overly literary ("chaffer," "behest") to the mundanely popular ("love-light in your eyes," "love-glow on your face," and "set my chilly blood afire"). Although the poem may seem overly melodramatic in a setting of scholarly analysis, it is not so in the context of real-life experience. Consequently, it has retained a measure of appeal.

On the whole, Fauset's poetry is derivative in content and form; and although one recognizes that her love and command of the French language were genuine, her use of French phrases and titles in her poetry seems contrived. The poems seem intended to demonstrate their author's personal refinement rather than to gain appreciation for their own sake. Her self-proclaimed aim to tell "the truth about us" placed a similarly heavy burden on her fiction.[16] Angered by the preponderance of degrading stereotypes about Black life generally and Black women in particular, she wanted to show that Black people were everything the stereotypes said they could not be: intelligent and cultured, noble and respectable. The result was a strongly idealized portrait as distorted as the negative portrayals it attempted to displace.

Of her four novels, *Plum Bun* (1929) is by far the most successful. It features well-drawn scenes of Black life in Philadelphia and Harlem and even contains a cameo portrait of DuBois (called Van Meier in the novel). The heroine, Angela Murray, had never been content with the quietly respectable life led by her parents. She found Negro society in Philadelphia confining and was bored by the endless discussions of race. Her only satisfying experiences occurred on those occasions when she and her light-skinned mother went downtown and enjoyed the diversions reserved for Whites. While to her mother "passing" was only a convenience, to Angela it seemed the key to a far richer life.

After her parents' death, Angela moves to New York where she hopes to find broader opportunities to pursue her study of art. She allows people to judge her race for themselves, and when they decide she is White she does not correct them. Drawn into the bohemian circles of Greenwich Village, she is soon disappointed by the vapid attitudes held by her new associates. Fauset's depiction of White artists and intellectuals is scathing and caricatured. As a group they are immature, selfish, dangerously radical politically, and completely amoral. It is a portrayal apparently drawn from the pages of daily tabloids. Fauset does add one new wrinkle: the bohemians are as prejudiced as their less avant-garde brethren. Though Angela is convinced that her New York "friends" are in every way inferior to the young Blacks she had known in Philadelphia, she cannot resist the tantalizing promise of freedom embodied in Whiteness. She begins to adopt the manners and mores of the Village; she snubs the one obviously Negro woman in her art classes and embarks on an affair with a wealthy White socialite. Inevitably, the affair turns out badly, and Angela eventually gives up her "White" status to take a stand on behalf of her Black classmate.

As a study of "passing," *Plum Bun* can be described in terms of established conventions. "Passing" is an immoral practice, as obnoxious to Blacks as to Whites. The "tragic mulatto" is doomed to a life of deception, continual fear of discovery, and lack of fulfillment. No honest relationships are possible on either side of the color line. Fauset does not indict "passing" solely on these grounds. Angela Murray can be forgiven all the things she does in her effort to achieve her goals, even the affair, which is conveniently forgotten once she reclaims her race. What she cannot be forgiven is her rejection of her sister, whom she declines to acknowledge when doing so threatens her relationship with her lover. Her disavowal of her sister is tantamount to rejection of self, and that is the unpardonable sin.

In *The Chinaberry Tree* (1932), her weakest fiction, Fauset's message to Black women is reduced to its barest essentials. A suitor's admonition to his girlfriend Melissa—"Be a good girl, a really good girl all the time"—echoes through its pages. Melissa is baffled by the warning and so is the reader since the girl, though immature and silly, never considers deviating from her strict moral code. But one understands that the explanation lies outside the confines of the novel. What Fauset is intent on proving is that most Black girls are good, most Black people are moral. Her sermonizing weakens the novel, but her primary goal, as always, was less to write quality fiction than to tell "the truth about us." One assumes she felt she had done so. However, her defense of her sisters' virtue seems both shrill and patronizing. Fauset failed to question prevailing standards of morality—as of literature—before seeking to prove how well Negroes were conforming to them. The training of the Methodist parsonage, Cornell, and the bourgeois social circles of Washington and Harlem had bred acceptance, not skepticism.

The failure of Jessie Fauset's fiction is not, as is sometimes suggested, that she chose to depict the lives of the small, elite segment of the Black community she knew best. It is rather her inability to step far enough away from the experiences of her group to write about them objectively. Although she was widely educated, Fauset drew on extremely conservative models for her fiction. The genteel novel proved a poor medium for the truth she tried to tell. Ironically, it could not encompass the truth of Fauset's own exceptional personal experience. So she took refuge in the more sensational stories of "passing."

In many studies of the Harlem Renaissance, the names of Jessie Fauset and Nella Larsen (1893-1964) are closely linked. They are said to belong to the "rear guard" of the period, the keepers and defenders of the Black middle class. In some respects the style of their personal lives was similar. Like Fauset, Larsen was part of that elite group of Blacks, well educated and financially secure, whose posture was—in critic Hoyt Fuller's sardonic phrase—"aggressively bourgeois." [17] In dress, manner, and language, there was little to distinguish them from their White counterparts. Yet perhaps because she lacked Fauset's family connections, Larsen always remained somewhat estranged from the clannish Harlem bourgeoisie. Moreover, she scorned purpose novels, just as she scoffed at the often sententious rhetoric of racial uplift. She was attracted instead to psychological fiction and created characters who were far more complex and believable than Fauset's. Although it was little understood by her contemporaries, Larsen was as interested in exploring the effects of sexism as of racism; thematically, her writing remains remarkably fresh.

The daughter of a Danish mother and a West Indian father, Larsen was raised in an intolerant Chicago immigrant community whose inhabitants had quickly assimilated the racist attitudes of their adopted homeland. She learned early to depend only on herself and to suspect the motives of everyone else, including family. She was well into her teens when she was first confronted with an all-Black environment at Fisk University, and the encounter was evidently unpleasant. She must have felt herself an outsider in Nashville, as she had before in Chicago and would again wherever she went. However painful such a situation was personally, it had its advantages for a novelist. Larsen became an astute observer, inclined to question the presumptions of all the groups with which she came in contact.

After her year at Fisk, she spent three years with relatives in Denmark, continuing her education at the University of Copenhagen. When she returned to the United States, she settled in New York City and studied nursing. Deciding again to cast her lot with Black America, she took a job as head nurse at the Tuskegee Institute. She was thoroughly disillusioned and enraged by conditions there; Tuskegee students were schooled in docility and subservience in addition to their academic subjects. Larsen soon returned to New York where she decided to change her profession from nurse to librarian. This new career brought her to Harlem and an association with the New Negro intelligentsia. These diverse experiences gave her a unique perspective from which to assess the condition of Black women—especially the educated middle class—in Western society.[18]

Nella Larsen's two novels explore the choices available to those relatively privileged Black women. Superficially broad, they were profoundly constrictive. In *Quicksand* (1928), the protagonist Helga Crane attempts first to devote herself to the policy of uplift practiced at Naxos, a fictional institution based on the Tuskegee model. But she cannot accept the school administration's belief that to be accepted, Blacks must deny their personal individualism and their cultural differences. Later in Chicago, Mrs. Hayes-Rore, a professional "race" woman, comes to Helga's aid; the reader's reactions to this woman are ambivalent. Mrs. Hayes-Rore is on the one hand considerate and sympathetic to Helga's plight, but on the other she is single-minded and pretentious. As it turns out, these same failings afflict most of the people Helga subsequently meets in Harlem. Although she is fond of their smart clothes and conversation, Helga finds the young Harlemites shallow and provincial. They are possessed of a race consciousness at once consuming and superficial, proud and ineffectual. Helga sees the limitations of their stance too clearly to adopt it. Because she comes into a considerable sum of money, Helga is able to withdraw from the American Black community and test the options available to her in Europe. They too are limited. Although she enjoys a greater measure of physical freedom in Copenhagen than in the states, she has less spiritual freedom. She is constantly on display, the object not of hatred or bitterness but curiosity. Unwilling to remain a novelty, she leaves Denmark. Returning to Harlem, Helga discovers that she has pretty much exhausted her options. Acting out of passion and desperation she marries the Reverend Pleasant Green, an illiterate Alabama preacher who appears to offer sexual and spiritual salvation. In her new-found religious and sexual fervor, she finds it easy to glorify the unlettered rural folk. She sees in their lives not resignation, but a mastery of the complexities of living. Only after her passion is spent is she able to recognize that she is incapable of emulating even those qualities she admires—the sustaining faith, the ability to cope with the unjust as well as the unexpected, the humor and hope she had earlier imagined she would find. And, of course, she discovers much that cannot be romanticized: the intransigence of poverty and racism, the lack of resistance from the folk, the particular oppression of women. To her horror, she finds she is no more able than her neighbors to extricate herself from this environment, and at the novel's close she is resigning herself to a fifth pregnancy.

Many critics have seen in Helga Crane an embodiment of W.E.B. DuBois's concept of the "double consciousness" afflicting Black Americans. This reading is encouraged by Helga's mulatto identity and by DuBois's enthusiastic praise of the book.[19] Other writers, notably James Weldon Johnson in his novel *The Autobiography of an Ex-Colored Man* (1912), had used a mulatto protagonist in fictional representations of the dilemma DuBois defined. Larsen, like most educated Blacks of the day, was almost certainly familiar with DuBois's often-quoted pronouncement:

> After the Egyptian and Indian, the Greek and Roman, the Teuton and Mongolian, the Negro is a sort of seventh son, born with a veil, and gifted with second-sight in this American world, a world which yields him no true self-consciousness, but only lets him see himself through the revelation of the other world. It is a peculiar sensation, this double-consciousness, this sense of always looking at one's self through the eyes of others, of measuring one's soul by the tape of a world that looks on in amused contempt and pity. One ever feels his twoness—an American, a Negro; two souls, two thoughts, two unreconciled strivings; two warring ideals in one dark body, whose dogged strength alone keeps it from being torn asunder.[20]

In keeping with this premise, Larsen's protagonist is unable to see herself clearly, even as she is unusually perceptive in her assessments of others, whether they be Black do-gooders at Naxos, White bohemians in Harlem, Copenhagen socialites, or her own family in Chicago. Her problem is an inability to accept the White world's definition of a Negro; she knows she is neither exotic nor primitive, "savage" nor sharecropper. Negroes' definitions of themselves are equally unsatisfactory, for they too are dependent on the White world's images. By either denying or exaggerating differences, Blacks are left with, in DuBois's phrase, "no true self-consciousness." This certainly describes Helga Crane's plight at the end of *Quicksand.*

This is only a partial description of Helga's situation: it ignores the female dimension Larsen clearly insists upon. This dimension signifies much more to current readers than it did to Larsen's contemporaries. Helga Crane is victimized by social definitions of womanhood as much as those of race. Her decisions to leave Naxos, Harlem, Copenhagen, and again Harlem are all prompted by the reactions of men with whom she is in some way involved. At Naxos she has been engaged to the son of a prominent Black family. James Vayle, of course, wants to marry a "lady," and Helga is uneasily aware that she lacks the proper pedigree. The child of a White mother and Black father who may not have been legally wed, Helga attributes part of her unease to her family background—but not all. "She was, she knew, in a queer indefinite way, a disturbing factor. She knew too that something held him, something against which he was powerless. The idea that she was in but one nameless way necessary to him filled her with a sensation amounting almost to shame. And yet his mute helplessness against that ancient appeal by which she held him pleased her and fed her vanity—gave her a feeling of power." [21] Here is an incipient realization that sexuality is political; it is power. But she mistakenly assumes it is hers to wield. She is entrapped by the need to repress her sexuality, to assume the ornamental, acquiescent role of "lady," which not only Vayle but the entire Naxos community expects. Her reflection that "to relinquish James Vayle would most certainly be social suicide" (p. 35) is followed by a scene in which Larsen develops one of a series of metaphors of suffocation and asphyxiation which thread through the novel. Revealingly, the words which force Helga's actual departure are not spoken by Vayle, but by another man, the "apparently humane and understanding" Robert Anderson who argues that she is needed there because "you're a lady" (p. 50).

Both Vayle and Anderson reappear in the Harlem sequences of the novel, thereby demonstrating that expectations for women remain the same. In Harlem Helga lives with Anne Grey, a wealthy widow whose elegant taste in clothes and furnishings largely define her character. Helga supposes that in order to indulge her own considerable proclivity for fine things she too must acquire a successful husband. But she is too repelled by Anne's calculation and cynicism to emulate her. That she cannot bring herself to reject Anne totally presages her fate. Helga wishes only to escape from Harlem; the five thousand dollars in conscience money paid by her White uncle provides the means to that end.

In Copenhagen Helga is courted by Axel Olsen, a portrait painter who sees in her the personification of the exotic primitive. Olsen eventually proposes marriage, but only after his suggestion of an affair has been ignored. In his proposal, Olsen makes explicit the connection between prostitution and marriage that Larsen implies when Helga considers marriage as a means to acquire things. Olsen declares: "You have the warm impulsive nature of the women of Africa, but my lovely, you have, I fear, the soul of a prostitute. You sell yourself to the highest buyer. I should of course be happy that it is I. And I am" (p. 149). Helga angrily rejects Olsen, but his accusations linger and influence her behavior upon her return to Harlem. She impulsively offers herself to Robert Anderson, now Anne Grey's husband, and he declines. The novel's "downward spiral" accelerates; the metaphors of asphyxiation multiply.[22] A drunken Helga stumbles into a storefront church and soon after into the arms of the Reverend Pleasant Green, who, true to his name, provides a retreat from thought and challenge as well as sexual refuge. By the time Helga analyzes this final choice, she is helpless to undo it.

Larsen's second novel, *Passing* (1929), has usually been described as the best fictional treatment of its very minor subject. Two characters, Irene Redfield and Clare Kendry, dominate the novel; both are attractive, affluent, and able to "pass." Irene identifies with Blacks, choosing to "pass" only for occasional social convenience, while Clare has moved completely into the White world. The trite plot unfolds: Clare, seeking thrills as much as identity, begins to make furtive trips to Harlem. Her White husband eventually follows and discovers her secret. Clare Kendry falls through a window to her death. However melodramatically, Larsen continues to survey the options open to supposedly privileged women and finds them wanting. So much energy devoted to keeping up appearances—as though their lives depended on it. Clare's life clearly did, and for others, relying on husbands for fine things, security, even identity, keeping up appearances was serious business indeed.

Genuine though it was, Larsen's talent bore relatively little fruit. Despite the critical success of her two novels and the Guggenheim Fellowship she was awarded in 1930, she subsequently published only one short story. Any number of nonliterary reasons have been proposed for Larsen's silence; intriguing though they are, they are so far unverified.[23] That she had not solved several key literary problems is demonstrable. In both novels, Larsen's style is disturbingly flat, the dialogue often painfully stilted. On occasion the language is so studied in its sophistication that the characters sound like actors in a drawing room drama. When Larsen expanded the perimeters of her fiction beyond the insular middle-class world, her failure to accurately reproduce speech made her Alabama peasants unconvincing. A more fundamental problem is her inability to transcend the inhibiting convention of the "tragic mulatto." In *Quicksand,* where Helga's racial identity serves a thematic function as an emblem of "double consciousness," Larsen is able to work within the convention without being overwhelmed by it. In *Passing* though, where Clare Kendry's situation follows the pattern of the convention—the victim caught forever betwixt and between until she finds in death the only freedom she can know—the inevitable melodrama of the "tragic mulatto" weakens the credibility of the narrative.

Clearly, attempting to work within stereotyped modes was dangerous. Moving beyond them was no less difficult. Creating characters possessed of "true self-consciousness," who were not merely self-conscious, was problematic for writers who themselves were pressured to meet the diverse and often conflicting demands of their Black public, their White public, and their art. It is therefore surprising that so much reflective of the reality of Black women's lives is present in their work. To discover the broader dimensions of Black women's reality, however, one must turn to an art born from folk culture and perfected by women who had liberated their creative powers. I speak of course of the blues.

It is impossible in this limited space to do justice to the achievement of the many blues singers whose careers flourished during the 1920s or even to discuss in any detail the accomplishment of universally recognized women. But a brief consideration of the artistry of Bessie Smith (1896-1937) will illustrate the point. For the literary minded, the most accessible approach to the blues is often through the language, a recognition of the blues as lyric poetry. Here Bessie Smith's poems provide a striking contrast to the work presented earlier. Take for example the well-known "Young Woman's Blues" written by the singer at the height of her career:

> *Woke up this mornin' when chickens was crowin' for days*
> *And on the right side of my pilla my man had gone away*
> *By the pilla he left a note reading I'm sorry Jane you got my goat*
> *No time to marry, no time to settle down*
> *I'm a young woman and ain't done runnin' round*
> *I'm a young woman and ain't done runnin' round.*
>
> *Some people call me a hobo, some call me a bum*
> *Nobody knows my name, nobody knows what I've done*
> *I'm as good as any woman in your town*
> *I ain't high yeller, I'm a deep yella brown*
> *I ain't gonna marry, ain't gonna settle down*
> *I'm gonna drink good moonshine and run these browns down*
>
> *See that long lonesome road*
> *Lord, you know it's gotta end*
> *I'm a good woman and I can get plenty men.*[24]

The poem's language and references immediately define the speaker and her setting as Black and Southern. Her tone expresses a complex mixture of bravado and vulnerability. She is a woman who, though resigned to life's broken promises and disappointments, refuses to let them defeat her ("I'm a young woman and ain't done runnin' round"). Still, she is painfully aware of the judgment the world assigns; "hobo" is most assuredly a euphemism. In the end she draws strength only from an implicit faith that the future is not as bleak as it appears—the long lonesome road must only *seem* endless. In the meantime she boasts of her ability to attract new lovers; it is the only boast she can make. She pledges to take joy where she can find it, and her words condemn a world that offers so little. Musicologist Ortiz Walton has written that "the blues as lyric/sung poetry is a medium through which passes the essence of the life experience, both its travails and its ecstasies."[25] The truth of this statement is verified when one listens to Bessie Smith's recording of "Young Woman's Blues," which despite its lyric is anything but despairing. When she sings "I'm gonna drink good moonshine and run these browns down," the listener recognizes that life's pleasures though transitory are nonetheless real.

One of the finest examples of the power of Smith's art is her much celebrated "Backwater Blues." It further illustrates her ability to capture in song the collective experiences of her people.

> When it rains five days an' de skies turned dark as night
> When it rains five days an' de skies turned dark as night
> Then trouble taken place in the lowland that night
>
> I woke up this mornin', can't even get outa mah do'
> I woke up this mornin', can't even get outa mah do'
> That's enough trouble to make a po' girl wonder where she want go
>
> Then they rowed a little boat about five miles 'cross the pond
> They rowed a little boat about five miles 'cross the pond
> I packed all mah clothes, tho'owed 'em in, an' they rowed me along
>
> When it thunder an' a-lightnin', an' the wind begin to blow
> When it thunder an' a-lightnin', an' the wind begin to blow
> An' thousan' people ain't got no place to go
>
> Then I went an' stood up on some high ol' lonesome hill
> I went an' stood up on some high ol' lonesome hill
> An' looked down on the house where I used to live
>
> Backwater blues done cause me to pack mah things an' go
> Backwater blues done cause me to pack mah things an' go
> Cause mah house fell down an' I cain' live there no mo'
>
> O-o-o-oom, I cain' move no mo'
> O-o-o-oom, I cain' move no mo'
> There ain' no place for a po' girl to go[26]

In addition to the graphically depicted situation, Smith's poem brilliantly evokes the speaker's mood of horror and amazement: "Cause mah house fell down an' I cain' live there no mo'." The moan is the acknowledgement of a desolation too profound to be verbalized. Although most of Bessie Smith's blues were love lyrics, "Backwater Blues" demonstrates her ability to handle diverse subjects masterfully. One cannot imagine any of Smith's sister poets attempting a subject of comparable magnitude.

For the blues she wrote herself, Bessie Smith drew on the common store of blues lines; in several instances, such as the two cited above, she created distinctive and personal poetic statements. Despite her not inconsiderable verbal artistry, Bessie Smith's reputation rests on her achievement as a performer, not a poet. According to her biographer Chris Albertson, Smith had vocal abilities no one in her field could equal, and she had a gift for showmanship to match. She sang, danced, and did comedy routines with a skill that was the envy of other performers. Appearing in tent shows and vaudeville houses, Smith had to give her audiences more than the blues. She frequently shared a bill with Black-faced comedians, dancers, jugglers, and any other specialty acts that won the public's favor. During the peak years of her career, she organized a troupe to satisfy the varied tastes of her fans.[27] But when called upon, she could meet all their expectations herself. An extraordinary contralto power was her greatest asset. She knew how to manipulate it with great subtlety, and her phrasing was the most sensitive of all blues singers. Despite artistic command of her "instrument," Smith could not always control the way it was used. In recording, she was frequently assigned material and accompanists by record company executives. A commercial success, Bessie Smith managed both to achieve stardom and maintain the integrity of her art.

Her audiences kept her honest. Their multifarious tastes to the contrary, they recognized the spiritual aspect of her work. Time and again, observers testified to the kinship between the revival tent and the tent show. A typical comment came from one of Smith's musicians: "If you had any church background, like people who came from the South as I did, you would recognize the similarity between what she was doing and what those preachers and evangelists from there did, and how they moved people. Bessie did the same thing on stage."[28] In part this was the result of Smith's celebration of a shared experience, a collective reality. The thousands who flocked to hear her rendition of "Backwater Blues," certainly including people who had themselves been left homeless by the record-breaking floods of 1927, heard in her music a witness to their own will to survive. As Ralph Ellison has eloquently stated: "Bessie Smith might have been a 'blues queen' to the society at large, but within the tighter Negro community where the blues were part of a total way of life, and a major expression of an attitude toward life, she was a priestess, a celebrant who affirmed the values of the group and man's ability to deal with chaos."[29]

The raw material from which Bessie Smith refined her art was alien to the other women so far discussed in these pages. Daughters of the Black middle class, they knew little of the folk culture and what they did know they had been trained to deny. They abhorred the raunchiness so much a part of Bessie's public persona, and unlike her audiences, could hear nothing of the spirituality or the art in her work. The one literary woman who was free to embrace Bessie's art, who was also heir to the legacy she evoked, was Zora Neale Hurston (1901?-60), for whom Ellison's words are no less appropriate. She was indeed a celebrant who affirmed the values of the group and man's (woman's) ability to deal with chaos.

In a period when many Afro-American male intellectuals hoped to immerse themselves in the Black folk tradition, Zora Neale Hurston represented that tradition in the flesh. Born in the all-Black town of Eatonville, Florida, she was one of the few renaissance figures to know the rural folk experience firsthand. The stories, superstitions and songs of her childhood remained a vital part of her experience and informed everything she wrote: short stories, essays, folklore studies, plays, and novels. Hurston had studied anthropology at Barnard, and she liked to describe herself as "a literary anthropologist." Aesthetically through her fiction and scientifically through her ethnological studies, she sought to communicate the beauty and complexity of Black folk life. The stories she published in the 1920s, her first two novels, and the book of folklore *Mules and Men,* all recreated the world she had known in Eatonville. It was a world she wanted to explain and celebrate. Hurston described the rural customs and folkways with affection and respect. Drawing on Southern Black speech patterns, she shaped a literary language rich in wit and metaphor. Of particular interest in her fiction are the vividly realized female characters distinguished by their independence, inner strength, and common sense. Hurston believed she had discovered a set of characters and situations unexplored in American literature. In her best work, she made them come alive in the reader's consciousness. Privately, Zora Hurston was an intense, dynamic woman who found it increasingly difficult to play the roles society imposed on her color and sex. Her behavior, especially during the Harlem Renaissance years, can most aptly be described by the Black English word *bodacious.* Needless to say, it sometimes evoked confused and bitter reactions from her fellows.

The 1920s were years of apprenticeship for Zora Neale Hurston. In courageous pursuit of the education she believed would free her, she was in 1920 a student at Howard University. Hurston had to work to support herself, and she could only attend classes intermittently. Nevertheless her talent and vibrant personality attracted the notice of Alain Locke, professor of philosophy, Rhodes Scholar, and a major catalyst of the nascent New Negro movement. Locke invited her to join The Stylus, a select campus writing club. The literary training at Howard inspired her to develop a voice but provided few useful models. Her first story, "John Redding Goes to Sea," was plainly amateurish; still Charles Johnson, editor of *Opportunity,* recognized Hurston's potential and asked for more material. She sent him "Drenched in Light," which became her first published piece.[30] The story describes an encounter between an innocent and vivacious little Black girl and a somewhat jaded White couple. The woman is pleased, because "I want a little sunshine to soak into my soul. I need it." And the girl Isis is happy, because "for the first time in her life, she felt herself appreciated." [31] While one can accept Isis's happiness at feeling "understood," it seems incumbent on Hurston to point out the limitations of this new understanding. Instead she seems oblivious to them. On another level, "Drenched in Light" echoes an attitude common in the twenties: Blacks in their childlike simplicity and gaiety could restore to Whites their seemingly lost capacity for joy and unencumbered emotion. Hurston, by drawing a child character, makes the myth somewhat less patronizing, but the artificiality of the story reflects the basic wrongheadedness of the idea.

Hurston's situation was inherently problematic. She had a sincere commitment to express the moral and aesthetic value of the folk culture that had nurtured her youth. Superficially, the *Zeitgeist* of the twenties welcomed a voice like hers; however, the prevailing myth of the exotic primitivism of Blacks distorted what she had to say. She persevered. Between 1925 and 1927 she wrote a series of short stories and occasional essays, all of which evince a consistent attempt to make her Eatonville experiences accessible to literature. The story "Sweat" is by far the best of Hurston's apprentice efforts. It prefigures several of the major elements in her mature work: the theme of marital conflict, a concern with the exploitation of Black women, a rural setting, and a liberal sprinkling of Negro dialect. Here no simplistic encounters between Blacks and Whites mar the credibility of the narrative, and Hurston invokes a reality that Bessie Smith's admirers would verify.

The protagonist Delia Jones is a laundress, the family breadwinner, and the object of much abuse by her husband, Sykes. Although the townspeople realize that the two are ill matched, "Dey never wuz de same in de mind." Delia meekly accepts his cruel treatment until he threatens to evict her in favor of a girlfriend. The threat strengthens Delia's resolve:

> She lay awake, gazing upon the debris that cluttered their matrimonial trail. Not an image left standing along the way. Anything like flowers had long been drowned in the salty stream that had been pressed from her heart. Her tears, her sweat, her blood. She had brought love to the union and he had brought a longing after the flesh. Two months after the wedding, he had given her the first brutal beating. . . . She was young and soft then, but now she thought of her knotty, muscled limbs, her harsh knuckly hands, and drew herself up into an unhappy little ball in the middle of the big feather bed. Too late now to hope for love, even if it

were not Bertha it would be someone else. . . . Too late for everything except her little home. . . . It was lovely to her, lovely.[32]

To further engage the reader's sympathy on behalf of Delia, Hurston stresses the lack of esteem in which the townspeople hold Sykes. "Sykes Jones aint wuth de shot an' powder hit would tek tuh kill 'em." They shun him and his lady friend. Although Sykes is at first taken aback by Delia's determination, he does not give up his plans. He decides to play on her fear of snakes and brings a rattler into the house. Despite Delia's hysterical reaction and neighbors' warnings that the snake is not properly caged, Sykes refuses to move it. The reader of course anticipates the story's climax, but interest is sustained. One sees how Delia's religious faith enables her to ride out the crisis, and there is an ample sampling of folk wisdom concerning snakes. The action is never hurried and the climatic scene is carefully drawn. As Sykes succumbs to his grim and horrible death, Delia feels a surge of pity but does not go to his aid. She stoically exacts her revenge.

Because of her style and subject, Hurston became associated with the so-called Young Turks of the renaissance. As one of their spokesmen, Wallace Thurman, explained: "They were interested in people who still retained some individual race qualities and who were not totally white American in every respect save color of skin." [33] Oddly enough, even among those who shared a like literary sensibility, Zora Neale Hurston's reputation rested upon her gifts of bon vivant, raconteur, and wit—as performer rather than writer. She loved to regale audiences with the songs and stories of Eatonville; Arna Bontemps would later remark that her performances became part of the lore of Harlem. According to Langston Hughes, she was "certainly the most amusing" of the Harlem literati. In his memoir, *The Big Sea,* he recalls how Hurston once moved into an apartment and asked her friends to furnish it for her. At the housewarming, realizing that she had forgotten to request forks, she proclaimed it a *hand* chicken party. On another occasion, finding herself broke as usual and late for a downtown appointment, she walked to a Harlem subway station. She was stopped by a blind beggar holding out his cup: " 'Please help the blind! A nickel for the blind!' 'I need the money worse than you today,' said Hurston taking five cents out of his cup. 'Lend me this! Next time, I'll give it back.' And she went on downtown." [34]

What is clear from the numerous "Zora stories" recounted by her contemporaries is that Hurston exemplified the Afro-American oral tradition. But while that tradition could mold the blues artistry of Bessie Smith, it was not in itself sufficient to sustain a literary voice. To become a creator as well as a performer, Hurston required an additional perspective. She found it in the study of anthropology. Upon enrolling at Barnard in 1925, Hurston had come under the influence of Franz Boas, the then preeminent American anthropologist. He and colleagues Gladys Reichard and Ruth Benedict gave Hurston a profoundly altered view of her Eatonville past. No longer were her Florida neighbors simply good storytellers, whose values were admirable, superstitions remarkable, and humor penetrating. As such, they had been well suited for local color fiction, but now they were part of cultural anthropology; scientific objects who could and should be studied for their academic value.[35] The impact of this revelation was stunning. Hurston had seemingly found her singular mission. She was the one who would locate the folkways of Eatonville in what Benedict would later define as "patterns of culture." Anthropology was the tool with which the apparently immovable contradiction which stymied other Black intellectuals including Locke, James Weldon Johnson, and DuBois—that Blacks were the same as other Americans, yet different—could be resolved.[36] In anthropology, the resolution was obvious. Particular cultural differences existed between Blacks and Whites, but all were bound in the same human condition. Blacks were neither exotic nor primitive. They had simply selected different customs from Benedict's "arcs of human behavior." By the time she graduated from Barnard in 1928, Hurston had done six months of field work, the preliminary research on which her pioneering *Mules and Men* would be based.

From 1927 to 1932, Hurston devoted all her energies to her work as a social scientist. She made long expeditions to Florida sawmill camps, Louisiana bayous, and Bahamian plantations, recording the folktales, songs, children's games, prayers and sermons, and hoodoo practices of the rural Black community. Hurston's writing conveys the extraordinary excitement she felt at being able to legitimize Black folk experiences from "shoutin' to signifyin'." Thrilled by her discoveries and impatient with the prolonged process of readying material for scholarly publication, she first presented the folklore in a series of theatrical productions. These concerts, variously entitled "From Sun to Sun," "All de Livelong Day," and "Singin Steel," were given throughout the country, and Hurston performed parts in them herself.[37] In an article, "Characteristics of Negro Expression," she had written that "every phase of Negro life is highly dramatised. . . . Everything is acted out." [38] In these productions, Zora Hurston the artist demonstrated the truth of what Zora Hurston the social scientist had observed. Through her performances she was able to lay claim to her material in a far more intimate way than the academic setting could have allowed. And while Hurston was steadfast in acknowledging the benefits of her university education, she refused to let her voice be imprisoned behind ivied walls.

In the 1930s, Zora Neale Hurston bore the fruit of her labors. In the beautifully crafted novel *Their Eyes Were Watching God*, she broke the psychological chains for all time. No longer mammies, mulattoes, or whores, no longer afraid they would be mistaken for same, Black women in literature could begin to be themselves.

NOTES

1. Langston Hughes, *The Big Sea* (New York: Hill & Wang, 1932), p. 223.
2. Alain Locke (ed.), *The New Negro* (1925; rptd. New York: Atheneum, 1969), p. 15.
3. Nathan Huggins, *Harlem Renaissance* (New York: Oxford University Press, 1971), pp. 227-43.
4. Elise Johnson McDougald, "The Task of Negro Womanhood." In *The New Negro*, ed. Locke, p. 370.
5. Countee Cullen (ed.), *Caroling Dusk: An Anthology of Verse by Negro Poets* (New York: Harper & Bros., 1927), pp. 74-75; Robert Hemenway, *Zora Neale Hurston: A Literary Biography* (Urbana: University of Illinois Press, 1977), pp. 22-23.
6. Arna Bontemps (ed.), *American Negro Poetry* (New York: Hill & Wang, 1963), pp. 22-23.
7. J. Lee Greene, *Time's Unfading Garden: Anne Spencer's Life and Poetry* (Baton Rouge: Louisiana State University Press, 1977).
8. Cullen, p. 47.
9. Nathan Huggins (ed.), *Voices from the Harlem Renaissance* (New York: Oxford University Press, 1976), p. 191.
10. Helene Johnson, "Poem." In ibid., p. 183.
11. Interview with Arthur Huff Fauset.
12. Hughes, p. 240.
13. Hughes, p. 218.
14. McKay, *A Long Way from Home* (1937; rptd. New York: Harcourt, Brace, & World, 1970), p. 112.
15. James Weldon Johnson (ed.), *The Book of American Negro Poetry* (New York: Harcourt, Brace, & World, 1931), p. 208.
16. See Marion Starkey, "Jessie Fauset," *Southern Workman* 61 (May 1932), pp. 218-19.
17. The term "rear guard" is taken from Robert Bone, *The Negro Novel in America* (New Haven: Yale University Press, 1965), ch. 5; Hoyt Fuller, "Introduction" to *Passing* (1929; rptd. New York: Collier, 1971), p. 18.
18. Adelaide Cromwell Hill, "Introduction" to *Quicksand*, by Nella Larsen (1928; rptd. New York: Collier, 1971), pp. 13-15.
19. See Huggins, *Harlem Renaissance*, pp. 157-59; W.E.B. DuBois, "Two Novels," *Crisis* 35 (June 1928), p. 202.
20. W.E.B. DuBois, *The Souls of Black Folk*, 1903; rptd. in *Three Negro Classics* (New York: Avon, 1965), pp. 214-15.

21. Larsen, *Quicksand,* p. 34. Subsequent page references will be made parenthetically in the text.
22. The phrase "downward spiral" is borrowed from Hortense Thornton. Her essay "Sexism as Quagmire in Nella Larsen's *Quicksand," CLA Journal* 16 (March 1973), pp. 285-301 was the first to emphasize the sexual dimension of Helga's experience.
23. Hill, pp. 15-17. Marital problems and disproven charges that Larsen's short story was plagiarized are among the reasons proposed.
24. Bessie Smith, *Nobody's Blues but Mine* (Columbia, recorded 26 October 1926).
25. Ortiz Walton, *Music: Black, White, and Blue* (New York: Morrow, 1972), p. 28.
26. Bessie Smith, "Backwater Blues." In *The Negro Caravan,* ed. Sterling A. Brown, Arthur P. Davis, and Ulysses Lee (1941; rptd. New York: Arno, 1970), p. 478.
27. Chris Albertson, *Bessie* (New York: Stein & Day, 1972), p. 24.
28. Albertson, p. 131.
29. Ralph Ellison, "Blues People." In *Shadow and Act* (New York: Signet, 1964), pp. 249-50.
30. Zora Neale Hurston, *Dust Tracks on a Road* (1942; rptd. Philadelphia: Lippincott, 1971), pp. 167-68.
31. Zora Neale Hurston, "Drenched in Light," *Opportunity* (December 1924), pp. 373-74.
32. Zora Neale Hurston, "Sweat." In *Voices from the Harlem Renaissance,* ed. Huggins, pp. 200-01.
33. Wallace Thurman, "Negro Artists and the Negro," *New Republic* (31 August 1927), p. 37.
34. Arna Bontemps, "Review of *Dust Tracks," New York Herald Tribune Book Review* (22 November 1942); Hughes, pp. 238-40.
35. Robert Hemenway, "Zora Neale Hurston and the Eatonville Anthology." In *The Harlem Renaissance Remembered,* ed. Arna Bontemps (New York: Dodd, Mead, 1972), pp. 190-214.
36. Huggins, *Harlem Renaissance,* pp. 137-89.
37. *Zora Neale Hurston: A Literary Biography,* pp. 175-85, 205-7.
38. Huggins (ed.), *Voices from the Harlem Renaissance,* p. 225.

Alice B. Toklas and Gertrude Stein. Photograph by Man Ray.

Library of Congress, Photograph Collection.

Edith Wharton.

Library of Congress, Photograph Collection.

Edna St. Vincent Millay. Photograph by Arnold Genthe.

Library of Congress, Photograph Collection.

Natalie Barney.

Princeton University Library, Sylvia Beach Collection.

Janet Flanner. Photograph by Berenice Abbott.

Sylvia Beach and James Joyce.

Margaret Anderson and Jane Heap.

Beinecke Library, Yale University.

**Georgia
O'Keeffe.
Photograph
by Alfred
Stieglitz.**

Jessie Fauset.

Library of Congress, Photograph Collection.

Ruth St. Denis and Ted Shawn.

PART III

Women in the Creative and Performing Arts

Introduction

World War I changed the nature of women's lives. More women worked outside the home while fewer servants were used to assist with housework. Mobility provided by the automobile and by women's greater sense of freedom was reflected in more casual dress, sports clothes, leisure and resort wear. Ready-made clothing became available. Women's clothing of the 1920s reflected lifestyles and attitudes that both men and women held about women. In the 1920s certain aesthetic shifts in women's dress, begun a decade earlier, took firm hold. Anne Hollander discusses the evolution of female fashion that led up to the look of the twenties, the way new styles and modes in art conveyed the look of clothing, and finally certain individual women, such as Gabrielle Chanel, around whom the decade's fashion look crystallized. The feminine image of the 1920s, the famous "flapper" look, provides a standard to which fashion still refers despite subsequent variations.

Arts in the 1920s were flourishing as never before, and with them theaters, movie houses, cafés, galleries, salons, and dance palaces. The arts were alive with a stir of experimental activity that reflected boundless exploration of the dramatic. Women and theater both came of age in the 1920s in America. Like women, theater gained the freedom not only to challenge nineteeth-century provincialism but also to create realistic and experimental dramatic forms, complex characterization, and lively speech. Women played a substantial role in all aspects of theatrical life, as actresses, playwrights, directors, and agents. Women's special role, Helen Chinoy states, was to serve the art rather than the business of theater. They founded drama leagues, published theater magazines, and formed theatrical groups devoted to performing plays that linked experimental theater with community life. In these theaters some of the more venturesome women dramatists exposed aspects of women's lives that had remained hidden from view. These plays expressed women's "suppressed desires"—their isolation, frustration, and troubled spirit—that had for so long remained secret. Women playwrights, such as Susan Glaspell and Sophie Treadwell, were important forces in unleashing these feelings. It is the voice of these women dramatists as well as the accomplishments of hard-working professionals, says Chinoy, that we seek to recover for women in theater today.

American theater gave rise to the first crusaders of dance as a modern theatrical art. Interpretive dance began as a uniquely American and feminine phenomenon that emphasized personal expression and feelings. This type of dance did not flower, however, until it was nurtured in the cultural capitals of Europe. Elizabeth Kendall traces chronologically the professional development and influence on dance styles of four American women—Loie Fuller, Ruth St. Denis, Isadora Duncan, and Martha Graham. Only the latter remained in America, converting the lyricism found in the dance of others into a "staccato modern song" to match the city and the geometry of her surroundings.

The stature gained by women in most artistic fields in the 1920s did not hold true for music. Ned Rorem examines this phenomenon stating that the evolution of music lagged behind other art forms. Music, although probably the oldest art, was the last to develop as personal expression. The twenties, he points out, were not rich in composers or performers of either sex; this was especially true in France, where emphasis on music was weaker than on the other arts. Rorem concludes that there is no women's art, but only art by women. He argues that too much emphasis is placed on *who* produces rather than on *what* is produced.

10.

Women and Fashion

Anne Hollander

Everyone knows what a "flapper" is. The word conjures an instant visual image of the characteristic look of women during the twenties. The flapper image is much more distinct that any other associated with a single decade in costume history. It seems to have sprung into being without antecedents and to have vanished without descendants—a unique image, outside the course of normal development in fashion. One reason for the sharpness of the twenties look in the mind's eye is self-consciousness about fashion during the period. The look of women, always important in society, seemed significant in a new way, and was being experienced and described as such more consciously than ever before.

After a long period of transitional modification in fashion, the decade was a period of artificially maintained extremes, during which certain new esthetic shifts in dress—changes in line, shape, and color which had begun a decade earlier—became congealed and confirmed in their final extreme version, and formed the basis of "classical" modern female clothing on which susequent modern fashion was to be founded. Although the shapes of dress alter continually and often change back again to old forms, some irreversible changes were admitted to occur during the 1920s—changes of slow genesis which had been in process since the turn of the century, but which seemed, at that intense moment after World War I and before the fall of the stock market, to come suddenly into focus. Certain views, established centuries earlier, of what women and women's clothes are always like remained in force during the twenties; but a much altered view of the meaning and workings of fashion and of the experience of women came into existence. During the decade slow changes in look, which occurred not much faster than in the 1820s or 1520s, were accompanied by a revolutionary shift in attitude which was much more radical than the visual changes and strengthened their effect.

The change in attitude and feeling accounts for the self-consciousness and self-descriptiveness of the period; there was new knowledge that the way clothes looked was central to the way life was lived. Women's clothes looked different, and people were studying the reasons for the first time. Clothes follow the flux of society, engaging in a constant creative symbolization of its ideals and conflicts. At any moment, women's clothes express attitudes about women held by themselves and by men, and especially about the bargain struck between the sexes concerning the visual expression of their relations. In the 1920s the terms of the bargain were acknowledged to have undergone a radical change. I shall discuss this whole subject in three ways. First, a comment about the evolution of female fashion that led up to the look of the 1920s—what the changes consisted of and expressed. Second, the way new styles and modes in art—painting, graphic, and photographic—conveyed the look of clothing at the time and influenced its perception then and since. Finally, to deal with certain individual women, working and living during the period, around whose names the look of the decade has crystallized.

Two important shifts of emphasis made women's clothes in the twenties radically different from the dress of the two preceding decades, even though the visual changes were gradual. The first difference was the postwar rise of youth as the vehicle of chic, with a corresponding revolutionary shift in the roles of mature and young women in the advance of fashionable dress. The Lady had gone out; the Girl had come in. The first real generation gap seems to have occurred. As often, mothers and daughters were deeply at odds, but this time daughters were winning out for the first time. The other difference was the rise of ready-made clothing, both in fact and on the social scale—not just the expansion of mass-production and standardization, but the *chic* of it.

Conventional modern attitudes about fashionable dress date from the establishment of these principles in the 1920s: that youth is the period of life in which to be in the avant-garde of fashion; and that basic commercial interests solidly and publicly support this point of view. Fashion then became and still remains a legitimate and glamorous business—dependent on the accurate gauging of fluctuations in youthful taste, seen to reflect the energy, hopefulness, even the conformity, insecurity, sexual crudity, outrageousness, and defiance of youth. The fashion business, established in the 1920s on a large scale, thus also simultaneously established extreme youth as a fashionable condition.

Just as exclusiveness and an emphasis on uncopiable individuality had characterized the productions of haute couture in the late nineteenth century, the quality of refined maturity had struck the fashionable note until World War I. Fashionably speaking, female youth was seen as a graceless period, gawky and awkward, undeveloped and unschooled, unequipped with sufficient confidence to carry off the serious and elaborate creations of haute couture. Grown women could have the skill and patience to manage complex garments and undergarments with ease, grace, confident sexual allure, and apparent effortlessness. Girls were impatient, wiggly and impulsive, and their figures had no style. Such attitudes naturally promoted the desire to look mature on the part of the young, rather than to look immature on the part of adults. Fashion had reflected this viewpoint about femininity for several decades during the nineteenth century; grown women had a great deal of scope in fashion for sexual expressiveness and conspicuous consumption, while young girls were something of an oppressed minority for which the ideal garments were sexually inexpressive, smaller in physical scope, and comparatively unadorned. When fast rebellious girls or very rich young ladies did wear ostentatiously elegant dress, it tended to imitate the full-blown look of maturity, to push toward that ideal: more décolletage, more trim, tighter stays. Fashionable mature women did not have the impulse to affect virginal shapelessness, schoolgirl simplicity, or playful childishness in dress.

Adult male dress was conceived on entirely different principles, trimmed and cut according to different esthetic rules and fabrics. The silhouette and spatial character as well as the texture and layering of male and female dress were entirely different during most of the nineteenth century; the symbolizing method was different in relation to the body. In the 1920s these differences were transformed and remodeled into a new relation.

World War I was the greatest influence on female fashion in the 1920s, chiefly because war's aftermath caused such an intensification and speeding up of change in women's lives and in the development of ready-made clothing. Other influences had also been at work before the war which determined the direction fashionable looks would take in their intensified form. Even without the war, hair would have been cut, breasts would have been flattened, waistlines would have been enlarged and displaced, and skirts would have been shortened. Female dress in general would have begun to take up less room and have less trim. All these changes had already demonstrably been wrought, at least at the level of high fashion, well before 1918. It was the swift popularization and visual exaggeration of these new elements in fashionable clothes which the 1920s accomplished, especially in the second half, as no decade had done before.

Mid–nineteenth-century feminine dress until the mid-eighties had become increasingly elaborate, colorful and decorative, even theatrical and excessively feminine, tending to stress the hourglass figure, great extent of skirt especially at the back, and great diffuseness of embellishment including the head. Feminine garments took up space and had an architectural structure and complex surface. The woman dwelling inside was inaccessible to the touch and extremely provocative to the imagination. Posture was upright, to support and display the hair and hat; the ribcage was lifted to thrust the bosom into prominence and keep the waist sharply defined above the very rhetorical skirt. Stays defined the correct shape, shifting according to changing mode. Besides trim, there were further extensions such as muffs, parasols, fans, bouquets, and so on.

As such details proliferated, dress-reform movements also arose and subsided. They raised consciousness, but not skirts, until they eventually had their cumulative overt effect in the twentieth century. The long struggle for female emancipation in England and America, also simultaneous with increase in fashionable excess, had lasting resonance in all feminine life. It could be ignored, but not unnoticed. Along with the rhetorical extremes of fashionable female dress in the nineteenth century came an underlying sense of their unseemliness and their preposterousness. Guilt and resentment, such as Freud was later to uncover, lurked under the ribboned and feathered hats and rows of graceful flounces, waiting for their moment.

As early as the 1880s, tailored skirted suits for women had come into vogue for daytime wear. Severe, businesslike, and practical-looking costume became newly chic for idle women for the first time—not just for riding and hunting, but for city wear. A decade later, the knickerbocker bicycling costume and simplified tailored dress for tennis came into fashion, expressing a new ideal of sartorial comfort for active sports. Both these changes were borrowed from the expressive elements in men's nineteenth-century clothing, increasingly severe for business and casual for sport during the course of the century. For women, these simplified garments, however severe or spruce, covered the body closely and were worn with stays and very high collars. Women's perhaps

unconscious emergent desire to be taken seriously required some echo-
ing of the masculine ideal of dress, although fashionable women's lives
changed very little.

Formal nineteenth-century male costume was just as physically cum-
bersome and constricting as female clothing. Trains, bonnets, and
whalebone stays were no more problematic than tall, stiff hats, layers of
lined and padded woolen tailored garments, mercilessly tight starched
collars, and ankle-high, tight-laced shoes. The design of men's clothes,
however, expressed the sense of physical articulation, and women's did
not. Between the sexes, the difference was not of physical ease. But
gradually for elegant women the look of severely cut discomfort came to
seem preferable to the look of fussy ruffled discomfort, at least for street
wear. Meanwhile, late–nineteenth-century female schoolteachers and office workers, plainly dressed often in ready-made garments, were still
not setting the fashionable tone. Nevertheless. the ideal of practical and
utilitarian-*looking* dress had come into existence as one important strain
in the modern development of female fashion.

At the turn of the century and especially during the first decade of
the twentieth, a marked reduction of both ornament and overall scope
occurred in elegant feminine clothes, along with marked change in the
shape and position of corsetting. The bosom was permitted to sink and
the ribcage to expand, while the corset descended to grip and mold the
hips and thighs, instead of the thorax. Posture, even more exaggeratedly
than the outmoded bustle, thrust out the behind. In front, the bosom
became very low and ill-defined, overhanging the stomach which
seemed to retreat. The back was still arched and the woman led with
her bust, as formerly. But even as early as 1911, the fashionable silhouette changed its basic form much more radically by a sharp shift in
posture. Suddenly the pelvis came to be thrust forward, the shoulders to
slump, the behind to tuck under and the bust to cave in.

This slouched posture became, though not all at once, absolutely
standard for fashionable modern female looks, and it has never lost its
appeal. The forward-thrusting hip, with hunched shoulders above, has
apparently successfully indicated elegance for the entire twentieth century, ever since it was crystallized into images by the artists working for
Paul Poiret between 1911 and 1913. At the time it was invented, this
look was a signal that stays were no longer essential to define the shape
of the torso: the well-defined waist and straight back were abjured for
the first time in a century and began to seem tacky; the female body
was seen to be most elegant when slumped. An interim fashion around
1910 kept the old posture, but enlarged and raised the waist and very
much narrowed the skirt, while keeping hats even larger. By 1913, the

narrow skirts were raised off the ground, hats reduced, and the slump established. Waists became blurry and legs visible.

In all this basic change, corsetting, officially absent, was all the more important because it now had the harder work of seeming not to be there. In the decade before World War I the corset had already become the hip-hugging girdle, made of elastic material with suspended garters to hold up the stockings. A bust-bodice, or brassiere, was worn above. Boning was still used, but to straighten rather than curve the figure. Women now needed help to look long, sleek, and slender, instead of hourglass-shaped. By 1915, the bust was sunken and minimal above a high waistline, and shoulders permanently slumped. The short skirt became fuller again, but shorter still; ankles appeared for good, and dancing became a pastime rather than an occasion. Harem skirts, first invented in 1911 for doing the tango, and causing a great furor, were a brief vogue which gave way to permanently short skirts—by comparison: they exposed the ankle and a few inches of leg. At the same time, the hitherto high neckline was lowered and opened for daytime wear to expose the neck and collarbones. Thus normal female clothing was reduced in the amount of room it took up and the amount of skin it covered well before the end of World War I.

These changes of shape, line, posture, and bulk occurred rapidly between 1910 and 1915, and created an essentially "modern"-looking female image, of which the most important aspect was undoubtedly the visible feet and legs. The new look made the head and feet of the female body come into visual relation with each other, so that the entire composition had to reduce proportionately to look harmonious. All extensions formed by clothing had to be smaller, trimming and head-gear had to reduce in scale and scope. Hair was cut off by some, bound close by most. The abstract silhouette, the reduction and simplification—the expressive style was becoming much more analogous to that of male dress. The design was not similar, but similarly allusive and abstracted, instead of fully worked out and embellished—like the difference between Neoclassic and Baroque architecture.

There were two main trends in all this which came into existence before 1920 and lasted until the middle of the decade. In the arena of high fashion in Paris, the trend was exotic, opulent and gaudy, shockingly vivid and erotic under the influence of Paul Poiret, Russian Ballet, and the residue of art nouveau. Erté and other famous decorative artists showed rather menacing serpentine turbanned figures festooned in drapes and dripping with oddly-placed pearls and tassels. Film vamps like Theda Bara in America took over this look. There were also bizarre street-wear versions with ospreys sprouting from hats and dramatic stand-up collars, worn with smoldering black-rimmed eyes. Simultaneously, a dainty and innocent aspect to feminine looks became possible by creating a childlike image out of the new shapeless body. Mary Pickford exemplified this trend in American movies. The vulnerable neck (now bare), the fluffy curls (now free), together with the short skirt, flat bust and high waist all lent themselves to a new look of attractive immaturity—not the attractions of a ripe young virgin but of a little girl. The implied sexual depravity of the predatory seductress was well matched and perversely echoed by the kind of sexual depravity implicit in the spectacle of the child-woman facing the wicked world in total ignorance of the power of her sex. These were Hollywood extremes; but they were definite elements in the new fashionable image of women, even in Paris.

Even before 1918, both these forms of feminine charm had the element of being physically accessible—the bodies of women, whether displayed as weapons or as prey, were dressed in a way to suggest that they could be grasped. The smaller scope of dress, the thinness of fabrics, and the elasticity of undergarments all contributed to this quality, furthered by the advance of couple dancing under the influence of Vernon and Irene Castle. A new use of fur, including whole coats made of it, also contributed to a new tactile immediacy in female dress. The physical distance between the sexes was getting shorter, as was the distance between the concepts of design governing their clothes.

The two exaggerated extremes of attractive female looks, the Child and the Vamp, generated by the new unstiffened leg-baring modes, thus combined before 1915 to challenge the sovereignty of the Lady, who went speedily out of fashion as an exciting sexual object. Mothers, trained to be ladies, found that daughters had no wish to carry on the tradition. Some carryover naturally persisted. It is interesting to see how démodé fashion art, using a fuzzy, sentimental, impressionistic technique, conveys this démodé, ladylike spirit in the second-rate fashion advertising of the time, while Erté and others were creating sleek linear abstractions to illustrate haute couture.

Then came the war. Women had to do the work of men, and they wanted and needed clothes that made them look as if they could do it. We have seen that the stirrings of such desires had already been expressed in dress much earlier in the eighties and nineties, in the form of severe tailoring; but they now had an excuse to come legitimately into play. Rich and elegant women, now short-skirted and uncorsetted, also had real work to do, which made practical-looking dress not an affectation but a necessity. Those who did no work had to adopt the look too, simply to look up-to-date. Simple, smocklike garments came into fashion, with big pockets and loose, serviceable belts. A quasi-military look became modish, as it always does in wartime. The trend in female dress was to divide clothes sharply between colorful, bare, soft evening garments (justified by the need to cheer the troops) and severe, practical daytime clothes suitable for driving a truck or working in hospitals. Egrets and chinchilla were now quite out of date for the street. The division between sexy, romantic evening clothes and plain, practical daywear is another modern notion, still in force, whereas during most of the nineteenth century and before the amount of trim, the complexity, and the degree of fragility in both day and evening clothes for women had been the same, although the forms of costume were different.

During the pretwenties and early twenties period of esthetic and moral change, certain assumptions about dress remained which were to vanish in the late twenties. The basis of couture was still exclusive, exquisite, and individual work. Fashionable clothing, although it may have become much simpler and freer, was still carefully made in conventional layers. Loose draperies were mounted on well-constructed linings, and many hooks and snaps affixed the festooning. Short skirts had slips beneath, and underwear was modest. There were still plenty of "ladies," and they still had the money. For them, a good deal of the modernized elegant dress remained sober, complicated, and delicate; gloves and hats were a matter of course. Ladies' maids were still in evidence, and the need for them was still obvious in the look of dress.

By 1920, briskness and practical simplicity for women's clothes were added by the atmosphere of war to the childlike and vamplike look. All three new modes could be visually compelling in the new relaxed postures and gestures already well established in a decade of fashion. They were soon synthesized and combined to create the feminine aspect of the later 1920s—the famous flapper look: part child, part vamp, and part competent good sport. Clara Bow sums it up in the movies. Masculinity was not part of the mixture at all, any more than ladyhood.

After the war, the twenties brought both "girls" and ready-made clothes into high fashion. The thin bodies, flat chests, and impulsive movements once thought to be lacking in any hope of style became the elements of extreme chic, along with the look of simple ready-made garments suggestive of the schoolroom and the tennis court even when they were made of chiffon. In 1921–22, fashionable women's hair was even more frequently bobbed, although Irene Castle had already done it several years before. In 1922, the fashionable waist had dropped to the hipline, although skirts were still just above the ankle where they had been for nearly a decade. Then in 1925 skirts rose to knee level for a short extreme moment; and sank to the ankle again by 1929. It was during those brief four years that the new feminine image acquired its final perfection and lasting fame. All the "modern" possibilities for female looks were at last firmly indicated: the visual possibilities for simple, abstract shapes in the design of women's clothes, analogous to those used in male dress; and the possibilities for reduction in the bulk of flesh and hair as well as of fabric, for exposure of skin and indications of bodily movements. The late twenties set a standard for all these, a standard to which subsequent fashion still refers, despite variations in feminine fashion since then.

Clothes at last took on real simplicity and "modernity," with minimal fastenings, underwear, and minimal cut, fit, and trim. The movements of the body were important, especially the legs and feet. Locomotion, not just dancing, was emphasized by the new half-exposed legs: they showed, as trousers had always shown, that their owner was going somewhere. In that sense women were at last the equals of men in expressing this particular aspect of the self-image. Visible leg movement, whether trousered or stockinged, means deliberate forward motion—personal progress.

In this country, stocking manufacture and consumption increased by 500 percent between 1919 and 1929; and 98 percent of the output was made of silk, a fiber formerly considered somewhat wicked and certainly unsuitable for everyday wear. Stockings were also and even more wickedly flesh-colored, for the first time. Great, moderately priced department stores began to flourish in America after the war; and the many young women in the work force who were spending their own money on ready-made clothes were setting the tone of fashion. The "poor look" was modish. The air of youth brought with it the air of classlessness, democracy, defiance of convention, and disregard for sacred old notions of exclusiveness, rank, and privacy as appropriate accompaniments to elegance.

Parisian fashion still depended on the exclusive work of great designers, not mass production, and Paris was still the fashion capital. Ready-made clothes were not chic in Paris until very recently; but the *look* of clothes which could be ready-made became very chic indeed—simple garments all very similarly cut, as men's had been for a long time. Yet even in America, Paris was looked to as the natural home of real fashion. Hollywood stars of the decade were dressed by Paris designers, and American department stores had salons for imported fashion. American designers existed to serve the ready-to-wear market, but their names were unknown; distinctive American designers emerged later in the thirties.

But in Paris in the 1920s, exclusive French fashion itself had gone public in a way unheard of before the war. This publicity, which became an essential element in fashion ever afterward, was accomplished in the twenties by an unprecedented alliance between haute couture and the press. Many fashion magazines of extraordinary glossiness and prestige came into existence in France. Showings of designer collections, once attended only by invitation and by private clients, were now publicly advertised and attended by journalists. Prominent women often wore couture models in public places to advertise the designer's work and were dressed free in exchange. Who made clothes for elegant women became news, publicly discussed in a way that would have horrified their mothers.

In this period Paris was also an internationally famous center of the arts. Art and fashion joined forces, now aided by the new art of fashion photography and the new magazines, and later assisted in this country by the popular art of film. The *Gazette du Bon Ton,* which existed between 1912 and 1925, was the first important magazine to unite art and fashion commercially and publicly. Paul Poiret and a group of excellent illustrators had created an abstract, stylized ideal look for the new modish woman as early as 1911, and this image was intensified in the hands of later fashion artists. The influence of painters like Modigliani, who died in 1920, was very strong on such illustrators as Georges Lepape, who illustrated Poiret's first volume of designs in 1908 and continued working for the *Gazette* and other journals. His elegant abstractions, like those of Erté, Benito, and Brunelleschi, were not perpetuating conventional styles of fashion illustration, but drawing upon the new forms of representation learned from Japanese prints, African masks, modern architecture, and serious painters—pursuers of cubism, futurism, and other new trends.

This visual alliance changed the nature of fashion. Fashion illustration in the last half of the nineteenth century had been related to the debased sorts of pictures on candy-box lids, not to the innovations of impressionism or fauvism. Women's fashion was thus implicitly a very minor art, a form of decorative frivolity. With the new link between serious and decorative artists, both of whose work appeared in the new magazines, combined with the advance of photography as an esthetic tool and the emergence of serious artists in the field of stage design and illustration, fashion became a suitable vessel for avant-garde esthetic expression. Fashion designers acquired great prestige—and incidentally, a great number of the best were women.

The connection between serious art and feminine fashion was not simply a matter of designers and artists being friends and influencing one another, but of the association going on in public view through the press and theatre. Fashion acquired an irreversible public importance in modern consciousness; and that is perhaps the most important contribution to fashion of the twenties, one which sharpened its image in historical consciousness. The art of the couturier achieved the prestige it has kept ever since, along with an implicit association with the other visual arts—not, as at an earlier date, an association with the more unfortunate aspects of feminine vanity and lack of serious purpose. One result of this association between art and fashion was to make the ideal image of woman—however free she was supposed to be in her skimpy clothes and short hair—into an artificial abstract shape, hard-edged, pictorially conceived, and emphatically unnatural. There were many fashion illustrators on a less elegant level still using the old methods—the fussy, sentimental, realistic graphic style consistently used for magazine illustration; but the most sophisticated fashion illustration, French or imitation, was abstract.

The abstract trend in modish looks shows up most significantly in the new use of makeup. No sooner were artificial hair and waistlines discarded than artificial faces came in. Kohl-rimmed eyes had come in with the vamp in the teens. In the twenties, in addition, lips and fingernails were vivid scarlet patches, eyebrows were thinly drawn lines, faces were sharp white ovals (until the vogue for suntan in 1927 made them sharp tan ovals in summer). The head and neck were meant if possible to resemble a Brancusi bust. The torso, although it may have been uncorsetted, was nevertheless ideally a stiff, unmodulated cylinder, and the cloche hat made a nonhuman-looking shape out of the entire head. The camera came to aid and confirm this stylization of the face and body by the end of the decade, although twenties designers still preferred the skilled stylizations of illustrators to the work of photographers for purveying the ideal look of their designs in magazines. The camera was still a bit untrustworthy; and women were still learning how to dress and move for it. Fashion photography came of age in the thirties, taking over the idealization of dressed looks. Fashion itself became more subtle, fluid, and susceptible to camera-lighting and vision.

A great assist was given to the establishment of a feminine photographic self-image by the movies of the 1920s. Operating some rungs below the level of the artists working for *Vogue* and the *Gazette du Bon Ton*, black-and-white cinematography in this country was beginning to govern our perception of ideally dressed humanity. For this function, camera art saw its flowering in silent film art before the end of the decade, in which the stylized dressed body appeared using the stylized expressions, gestures, and movements appropriate to its shape. Sharply

defined black lips and smooth waves of hair went with certain exaggerated facial manners, ways of using the hands, holding the shoulders,
and moving the hips. All these, conveyed in vivid black and white,
produced conventions for expressing feeling and undergoing experience
in what was seen as a "natural" manner. Clothes worn in these films
were emphatically designed, conventionalized so as to be understandable at a glance and look natural. The range of color was reduced to the
black-and-white spectrum. Contrast, line, texture, and movement had to
fill in for color and sound, exaggerated and stylized to seem sufficiently
real.

One lasting effect of the new-born cinematic vision of life was the
need for slimness. Fashion artists can draw figures as slim as they like;
the camera, moving or still, seems to fatten the figure. Movie stars'
figures, and ordinary ones conceived in imitation of them, had to become thin to keep their trim look under the camera eye. The modern
ideal of slimness we still uphold began not with the discoveries of
medical science but with the advance of camera consciousness in the
1920s. Before then, no matter how skinny Erté and Lepape made their
fashion figures in the teens, actual bodies were still visually acceptable
when quite hefty, as the stills of Theda Bara and others show. By 1925
most admired figures were slim, both in fashionable society and in the
screen community.

Slimness was also a part of the revolution in feminine physical ideals
which had been in process for a while but which only surfaced in the
postwar decade. During the prosperous period of nineteenth-century
ladyhood, there was an undercurrent of Romantic idealization of another kind of woman. While censuring her, society loved the image of
the doomed Camille, wasted by poverty and disease but still her own
mistress—wife to none, daughter to none, free in sexual choice, manager
of her own fortunes, and strong-minded and capable of noble sacrifice.
This heroine of nineteenth-century romanticism is echoed in the 1920s
character of Iris Storm from Michael Arlen's *The Green Hat*—another
doomed and frail adventuress. Thin Garbo played both parts, needless
to say. This sexually independent woman with such great literary appeal
was naturally thin—perhaps neurasthenic, ill, occasionally poor, but also
restless, searching, and deliciously nonrespectable. She was a huntress,
perhaps feral or sporting, or even virginal like Diana, but certainly not a
lady.

Thus besides the rise of sports and gainful employment, the new
knowledge of vitamins, and new practical aspirations toward sexual
equality in professional opportunity, there were old ideological forces

behind the new slim figure, having to do with the equal claims of female sexuality—its equal strength, its aggressive nature. Sexually predatory women must be naturally thin, since sexually passive ones are plump; the wicked vamp no less than the healthy tennis player contributed to the new image of desirable thinness. Thinness also implied that another aspect of female life had to be abandoned along with dependent daughterhood and passive wifehood; motherhood had to go by the board. Bellies, breasts and hips, erotic though they might intrinsically be, were too "healthy" for current tastes. Wantonness now had to find expression in lean serpentine bodies suggesting danger, instead of voluptuous bodies suggesting pleasure.

In 1927 hair was further shortened, and the shape of the skull and neck appeared. This, along with the new free-moving simplicity of dress, the air of aggressive sexual challenge, and of extreme youthfulness in feminine style, combined to produce a flavor not of girlishness (which is only a young version of ladyhood) but of boyishness—the famous *garçonne* quality. This mode was energetic and free, also somewhat depraved—one of the underlying characteristics of the "flapper." She was an unfamiliar kind of creature suggesting a naughty schoolboy ready for any kind of perverse experience, especially sexual; independent, adventurous, and daring, but still very much played off against men—rather like a thirteen-year-old male hustler. Real female independence was *not* expressed in the fashions of the twenties. The new look suggested the nonhuman vibrant sexuality of race horses and sportscars: an untamed, challenging organism in need of expert guidance—sleek, swift, and unaccountable—the madcap heiress ready to be subdued by the sheik. In this revolutionary period in fashion history women did not wish to resemble men in any tedious way suggesting responsibility and the management of serious affairs or hard practical work—such "mannishness" had been affected by women seeking emancipation in Victorian times. Speaking through fashion, feminine independence in the twenties was all on the surface, a matter of rhetoric just as pointed as bustles and tight lacing.

Certain women seem to sum up and stand for the look of the twenties in various ways. We mentioned Clara Bow as the one perfectly synthesized successor to the "child" Mary Pickford and the "vamp" Theda Bara. Gloria Swanson and Mae Murray would be among the list of potent Hollywood image models. There were noncinematic figures, however, that appealed to the popular imagination and trained the popular eye. Early in the decade (1922), for example, it was Suzanne Lenglen, the internationally famous French tennis star, who first wore a straight, sleeveless tunic with a knee-length pleated skirt and a headband. She struck that particular note of absolutely simple sportswear that became chic even in the ballroom and tearoom for the next few years.

In Paris in the middle of the decade, dress designer Sonia Delaunay represented the union of art and fashion by designing clothes as if they were paintings. She was the wife of a painter, and she used the currently geometric shape of the fashionable female body as a canvas on which to apply patches of color in asymmetrical patterns, similar to those painted on canvas by her husband and his circle. This direct juxtaposition, where a clothed body and a painting could be made into similar works of art, was perhaps only thinkable just in that decade. Sonia Delaunay's designs do not represent a real fashion trend; but they illustrate one extreme direction fashion just at that time could take, as it could have done at no earlier time.

The name with the most lasting resonance in the world of 1920s women's fashion is that of Gabrielle Chanel. Apart from her obvious talents, the reason for this is that she was the first couturière able to present her view of women's ideal looks and behavior in her own person. By contrast, Chanel's great contemporary Madeleine Vionnet, who was a modern genius at cutting and draping extremely simple clothes with utmost subtlety, stayed in her atelier and let her creations speak for her on the bodies of other women. Everyone knows what Chanel looked like; she was perpetually expounding and appearing as a living example of her theories. No one knows how Vionnet looked or what she wore, although her contribution to dress design was as important as Chanel's. Chanel combined the basic work of design with a role in fashionable life itself: she was not only a fashionable designer but a fashionable person, and the first couturière to be so. It was partly the postwar phenomenon of café society which made this possible. A complete breakdown of old conventions in social mixing allowed talented people of all sorts to be the accepted social companions of rich and titled people, instead of automatically being considered their servants and inferiors, and condescended to even while being admired.

Chanel was herself an independent, sexually free woman, a beauty, a professional success, intelligent, plebeian, tough, and *thin.* Apart from her designs, she was the first couturière to sell a complete modern image and show how to create it—not just clothes, but an air, a style, a way of combining things. While hobnobbing with the cream of society in France and England, as well as with the likes of Cocteau and Stravinsky, she advocated, adapted, designed, and wore clothes suggestive of working-class comfort and unpretentious ease, not glamorous leisure. She created and made accessible and visible new modern terms for the old "dandy" idea, best expressed by Beau Brummell in the early nineteenth century, that clothes while they are being worn should not seem to matter at all. This sartorial notion has an enduring and seductive appeal; it appeals to vanity as no other style of looks can because it visibly suggests that people are superior to their clothes without having to display any particular real superiority. Chanel's insistence on big, fake jewelry and mundane fabrics like jersey reflects an insistence on unpretentiousness, but also a recognition of crudity and coarseness in life—not just their existence, but their keen attractions and their ability to form compelling combinations with refined elements. Such a combination existed in her own personality, which in itself was such a success.

One of Chanel's other great contributions to the modern conception of clothes was the appealing idea that personal beauty is irrelevant to fashion. You make something marvelous out of yourself, whatever there is to start with. "There are no ugly women," she is supposed to have said, "only lazy ones." Corollary to this is another compelling idea that youth is also irrelevant, despite the trend of the moment. The kind of youthful and simple fashion she advocated could be extremely becoming to mature faces—her own being an increasingly excellent example as she approached middle age. Chanel was French, and women, not boyish girls, have always been admired in France. One reason haute couture could continuously flourish was that French women still required suitable clothes, and a segment of the international fashionable world still had an ideal of mature French elegance. There continued to be "ladies" throughout the twenties—adult women with high standards of personal elegance and high incomes.

Chanel's spirit of unpretentiousness also took the form of not minding being copied. She rightly saw imitation as a sign that a design was good, and she believed that a fashion was not good unless many adopted it. From her haute couture position Chanel was the first French designer to encompass and envision the way mass production could become the foundation of modern elegance. Now it is the choice and combination of manufactured objects that fashionable women engage in, and prestigious designers design for many; their clothes are manufactured, not individually cut and fitted, and their appeal even lies in the very scope of their suitability. The standardization of good looks which came about in the twenties and continues through the century, although it was made possible by the advance of manufacturing techniques and fostered by cinema, was originally given fashionable status partly by the influence of Chanel's views on her generation. Many other excellent designers of both sexes flourished in the 1920s, and many had similar conceptions. Chanel is an interesting innovative figure because she made use of her self-image as a living demonstration of her work and ideas; she was her own client and her own mannequin.

In contrast to the movie images of the decade, which appealed to popular taste, Chanel's message was aimed at the top; but one of her first principles was to destroy, among exclusive people, the notion of the exclusive look in dress—the look of having spent a lot of effort, money, and time being fitted. She was interested in what working women wore, what sailors wore, in the clothes of waitresses and seamstresses. She, working at the highest level of couture, caused the look of the youthful working woman to set the tone of fashion for the whole decade—perhaps for the whole century. She represented in her own looks, speech, attitudes, and behavior the essence of "modern" womanhood: feminine and sexy but not especially nice or eager to please, rich by her own efforts, uncompromising. She got where she was not just by talent, vision, hard work, but by using her sexual charm adventuress-style: she did not have a mission to be a great designer; she had lovers who set her up in business. She was an unstoppable combination of talented artisan, adventuress, and business woman—with no desire to hide her origins, methods, or qualities to masquerade as a fine lady even among fine ladies. Her clothes, worn by her or others, reflected this heady mélange. She showed how the new youthful look could be modified to create the image of a mature woman, independent, well at ease in modern adult life.

Femininity, in French mature form, perverse boyish form, or movie form, nevertheless remained unchallenged in 1920s fashions. Women wore dresses and hats, gloves, stockings, and heeled shoes. Schoolgirl-like sweaters and skirts were worn, but dresses were knee-length for tennis and bathing suits were modest. Fabrics were fragile, there were no "easycare" synthetics, and women and men's clothes were still sharply divided in design, but the sexes did achieve a certain equality in the conventional simplicity and physical expressiveness of their dress. All clothes seemed designed for easy movement of arms and legs; clothes of both sexes took up about the same amount of room and stayed close to the body without fitting very tightly anywhere. This nice balance first struck in the 1920s did not last past the thirties—another war and its aftermath had distorting effects on modern fashion. But the balance has been restored and recognized as one of the basic principles of twentieth-century dress. Chanel, who died in 1970 and worked until the end of her life, had a career which demonstrated her prophetic importance. She stopped designing and went into eclipse during the late forties and early fifties when complexly cut and artificially supported ladylike clothing came back into vogue. The last fifteen years of her life saw the general reestablishment in fashion of her notions of simplicity and informality, of separate simple garments with dramatic accessories. She went back to designing with enormous success. Chanel and the twenties had established the classically modern female way of looking which we still admire even with all its variations.

11.

Suppressed Desires:
Women in the Theater

Helen Krich Chinoy

American women and American theater both came of age in the 1920s. With the passage of the Nineteenth Amendment in the beginning of the decade, women were about to enter a new era. They would gain the freedom not only to vote but also to realize themselves more fully in education, careers, and most significantly in redefined social and sexual roles. Theater was also about to enter a new era. It would gain the freedom not only to challenge nineteenth-century provincialism and prudery but also to create realistic or experimental dramatic forms, complex characterizations of American figures, and utilize lively, even vulgar American speech. Little theaters devoted to art rather than show business would redefine the very idea of theater in America.

In the 1920s the theater in New York reached its greatest level of production. Never before or since has there been so much activity of such great variety—from the Ziegfeld Follies, to popular thrillers and farces, to new dramas of Eugene O'Neill, Elmer Rice, Maxwell Anderson, George Kelly, Philip Barry, and others that gave the twenties its distinction as America's first decade of mature, serious drama.[1]

Women played a substantial part in all aspects of this vigorous theatrical life. As always there were the actresses. Some of the old-timers like Mrs. Fiske and Ethel Barrymore were still active as new stars began to shine. It was the decade of Pauline Lord, Clare Eames, Laurette Tayler,

126

Katharine Cornell, Jeanne Eagels, Lynn Fontanne, Jane Cowl, Helen Hayes, and Eva Le Gallienne. No longer restricted to the roles of either the idealized heroine or the fallen woman, they gave the era a special glamor and brilliance as they played "flappers," sophisticated society women, small-town waitresses, and neurotic new women, as well as the heroines of Ibsen, Shaw, and Shakespeare.

As playwrights women made a new, secure place for themselves. The decade opens with Zona Gale winning the Pulitzer Prize in 1920–21 for *Miss Lulu Bett,* a spare, touching, Midwestern-genre depiction of an exploited spinster, dramatized from her novel. The decade ends in 1930-31 with Susan Glaspell gaining the Pulitzer Prize for *Alison's House,* her interpretation of the hidden love life of Emily Dickinson. The hit show of Broadway in the twenties was Anne Nichols' sentimental comedy *Abie's Irish Rose.* It ran for over five years, earned Anne Nichols a million dollars in royalties and millions more as producer of her own show, and was on its way, critic George Jean Nathan quipped, to becoming "the fourth biggest industry in the United States." [2]

One of the theatrical scandals of the decade was the production of Mae West's *Sex* in 1926. For the first time a play written by a woman was attacked as "crude" and "sensational," [3] and the cast along with its author-star were hauled off to jail. This helped the show have an impressive run of 375 performances. At the opposite end of popular taste, audiences enjoyed almost every year a play on a topical, frequently female theme by Rachel Crothers, who was to have the longest and most sustained career of any woman playwright—from 1906 to 1937. In all, over 150 plays of almost every variety were written by women for Broadway, the largest number of plays by women ever produced professionally in one decade.[4]

Many of these plays by women were irredeemable trash—on a par with most of the plays by men. Translations and adaptations of French farces and melodramas, for example, were something of a rage with women playwrights. If the original was French, it seems one could afford to be more risqué. Reviewing such a concoction, *The Masked Woman* by Kate Jordan in 1922, George Jean Nathan estimated that "in thirty-five years of this type of chasing a lovely pure girl around every available piece of furniture, the villain has covered 8,921 miles in pursuit to no avail." [5]

Despite the lack of quality of some of the plays, participation by women in the professional work of theater was a sign of the liberated spirit that brought us the vote and flappers. Much of theater had been closed to women in the nineteenth century, but by the turn of the new century some were complaining that theater seemed to be "for and by women." By the twenties a number of women were doing with success pretty much what men were doing. Writing of "Things Theatrical" in *The Woman Citizen* of December 1925, Kate Oglebay cheered that "now women are forcing their ways into all sides of the theatre . . . . They have become playwrights, pageant directors, workshop directors, play agents—a dozen specialized positions unknown to women a generation ago." Even the career patterns of women dramatists seemed to follow much the same shape as men's. Women journalists, in themselves fairly new, were turning from newspaper work to theater—Susan Glaspell, Edna Ferber, Sophie Treadwell, for example. A good number had prepared themselves as had Eugene O'Neill, Philip Barry, and Sidney Howard in Professor George Pierce Baker's famous playwriting courses, which had originated at Radcliffe and were indebted, as he himself acknowledged, to "feminine influence." [6] Hallie Flanagan, like Theresa Helburn, Agnes Morgan, and Maurine Watkins, a Baker student, became one of the first women awarded a Guggenheim Fellowship, which she used to study innovations in European theater.

This accommodation of women in the ongoing life of theater is best expressed in a 1926 manifesto of the Institute of the Woman's Theatre, an organization to which most leading actresses and playwrights lent their names.

> The Woman's Theatre is a group of successful professional women organized to promote women's work in the theatre and to render aid and give counsel to all who may apply. Whether she has a voice to be heard—a play to be read—a desire to act—or to paint scenery—whenever a woman asks our advice or seeks our aid in securing an audition, we assist her without charge. It is our desire to have our own theatre in the near future, to be managed entirely by women and feature plays written and directed by women. . . . We are not Pollyannas or reformers, but we do know that women will contribute something very worthwhile. . . . Women's influence in her own theatre, as indeed in any public activity, cannot but raise its standard.[7]

Important as these professionals were in making a place for women, they did not challenge—except by being there and being wholesome—the conventional values and forms of Broadway entertainment. However, just as women in the suffrage movement have been divided into compromisers and radicals, there was a similar division among women in theater. Off-Broadway and in the subscription and repertory theater women made a more challenging contribution: serving the art of theater rather than the business of theater has been the special role of women in American theater.

Women did much to prepare the way for a more significant American drama by founding the Drama League as early as 1910 and publishing their *Drama Quarterly* through 1931. It was a woman, Edith Isaacs, editor of *Theatre Arts Magazine,* who identified the need in the twenties for a "tributary theatre," a "native but universal creative theatre" that would have a "human and aesthetic relation to the life of the people." Women writers, directors, and actresses were active in the organizations that comprised this alternative theatre.[8]

Susan Glaspell was cofounder with her husband, George Cram Cook, of the Provincetown Players and wrote her plays especially for their stage. Also at the Provincetown Players were Nina Moise, a director who shaped some of O'Neill's first plays for the stage, the lyrical Edna St. Vincent Millay, and Ida Rauh, known as the Duse of MacDougal St. Irene and Alice Lewisohn organized the Neighborhood Playhouse where community life and experimental theater were linked. Their friend, Aline Bernstein, designed sets and costumes for their shows. Helen Westley and Theresa Helburn were on the governing board of the Theatre Guild, where the young Cheryl Crawford got her start. Eva Le Gallienne as star, director, and producer of her Civic Repertory Theatre on Fourteenth Street crusaded for popular-priced stagings of the masterpieces of dramatic literature as she trained a generation of young actors.

It was largely in these theaters that some of the more venturesome women dramatists exposed aspects of women's lives that had long remained hidden from view. On Broadway Rachel Crothers was tracing what she called "the New Woman's journey through her brave new world." [9] She did help shift the perspective of playgoers about women's role and the marriage bond, despite her conventional forms and her often conventional endings. Her *Mary the Third* in 1923 was a kind of social history of courtship and marriage in which each of three generations of Marys—grandmother, mother, and flapper granddaughter—is shown choosing her man. But off-Broadway more revealing insights about women were offered in experimental forms that seemed invented to express the troubled spirit of modern woman.

Alice Gerstenberg's *Overtones,* produced by the Washington Square Players in 1915 and widely played in the twenties, is viewed as the first American play "to depart from realism to show the unconscious." [10] She used the then-novel Freudian concepts of ego and id to dramatize the complex feelings of two women, each shown on stage shadowed by her alter ego, as they compete for a man and social position.

Susan Glaspell devised ways of getting at women's unconscious without abandoning realistic detail. Although her 1914 play *Suppressed Desires* was a comic takeoff on the fascination of the literary crowd with dream interpretation and psychoanalysis, the title of the play suggests the theme of women's isolation and frustration, which she was to make her central preoccupation in a striking group of plays in the next few years. In *Trifles*, her one-act masterpiece, she revealed in harsh detail the limited Midwestern farm life she knew so well. Two wives accompany their husbands to investigate the home of Mrs. Wright who is in jail for the murder of her husband. While the men inspect the murder site upstairs, the women examine the kitchen where the woman's life had been confined. There they find the telling trifles that reveal the motives for the murder. Understanding the loneliness and isolation of the woman and the brutality of her husband, they conceal their evidence from their husbands in a gesture of female solidarity. This little drama acquires great tension because the woman whose motives we are trying to understand never appears, a device Glaspell was to use in two other longer plays, *Bernice* and *Alison's House*. The absent woman in each of these plays is one whose true feelings had remained a secret to those around her. The discovery of her suppressed desires provides the action and meaning of the dramatic events. It was Glaspell's way of expressing her deep perception of female anguish and sacrifice.

In *Bernice*, the central figure has just died. Her wish to have her philandering husband think that she committed suicide controls the action and gets from the erring husband's guilt feelings the love and power she never had in life. In *Alison's House* the heroine, the Emily Dickinson figure, has been dead some eighteen years; the story of her love for a married man is revealed in the discovery of her unpublished poems. The poems tell the "story she never told . . . . The love that never died—loneliness that never died—the anguish and beauty of her love."

In *The Verge* in 1921 Susan Glaspell put her heroine directly on stage. The result is a most extraordinary, somewhat expressionistic play in which Claire Archer, an experimental horticulturalist, struggles to enlarge the boundaries of her life and experience. Her search for "otherness" and "apartness" leads her to the verge of madness and beyond. In rejecting home, husband, and child, and murdering her lover, she rejects the socially and biologically defined role for women. She exposes suppressed desires never before voiced by women in the theater. She implores her lover: "Let me tell you how it is with me; I want to touch you—somehow touch you once before I die—let me tell you how it is with me. I do not want to work. I want to be; do not want to make a rose or make a poem—want to lie upon the earth and know." "Do you think I'm just a fool or crazy," she asks him as her pained voice cries out: "Stabbed to awareness—no matter where it takes you, isn't that more than a safe place to stay?" With a reckless laugh she reaches out to the audience: "I'd be willing to take a chance, I'd rather lose than never know."

The anonymous young woman of Sophie Treadwell's 1928 play *Machinal*, like Glaspell's tormented but aspiring heroine, exemplifies the new image of woman. Although *Machinal* was produced on Broadway, it was brought out by Arthur Hopkins, the one commercial director-producer who had close associations with the art theater movement. Based roughly on the Ruth Snyder-Judd Grey murder case that Treadwell had covered as one of the country's leading women journalists, the play uses expressionistic sounds, rhythms, and images to suggest the "mechanical, nerve-nagging" environment that drives a very ordinary young woman to illicit love and the murder of her vulgar, fat husband, once her boss. In a stream of consciousness passage following the birth of her child, whom she rejects, she cries out: "Let me alone—let me alone—I've submitted to enough—I won't submit to any more." She confesses to the priest that the murder is the one free act of her life. As she is led to the electric chair, she again cries: "Leave me alone! Oh, my God, am I never to be let alone! Always to have to submit—to submit. No more—not now—I'm going to die—I won't submit."

It is the voice of these women dramatists and the accomplishments of hard-working professionals that we seek to recover for women in theater today. They left a legacy that has been long neglected. We need to explore it not only to set the record straight but also to help us make a new women's theater and to understand the experience of women in American life.

NOTES

1. Hyman Howard Taubman, *The Making of the American Theatre* (New York: Coward McCann, 1965), p.155.
2. Doris Abramson and Laurilyn Harris, "Anne Nichols: $1,000,000.00 Playwright," *Players Magazine* (April-May 1976), p. 124.
3. Phyliss Marschall Ferguson, "Women Dramatists in the American Theater, 1901-1940" (Ph.D. thesis, University of Pittsburgh, 1957), p.175.
4. This includes ten separate volumes which are part of a much larger series; one volume was produced each year. On the book itself the editor appears as Burns Mantle; for bibliographic purposes his name is Robert Burns Mantle. The title of each volume begins *The Best Plays of . . .* (only the year changes). The publishing house changed in the mid-twenties. (Robert) Burns Mantle (ed.), *The Best Plays of 1920-21* (Boston: Small, Maynard, 1921); (Robert) Burns Mantle (ed.), *The Best Plays of 1925-26* (New York: Dodd, Mead, 1926).
5. Ferguson, p.153.

6. Wisner Payne Kinne, *George Pierce Baker and the American Theater* (Cambridge, Mass.: Harvard University Press, 1954), p.154.
7. "Institute of the Woman's Theatre" (New York: Museum of the City of New York, Theater Collection brochure, 1926).
8. Edith Juliet Rich Isaacs, "The Tributary Theatre," *Theatre Arts Monthly* (September 1926):567-79 passim.
9. Rachel Crothers quoted in I. Abrahamson, "The Career of Rachel Crothers in the American Theatre (Ph.D. thesis, University of Chicago, 1956), p.70.
10. David W. Sievers, *Freud on Broadway* (New York: Hermitage House, 1952), p.32.

12.

Women and Dance

Elizabeth Kendall

Dancing as a modern theatrical art was still a new thing in the twenties, only a generation old. It was first perceived around the turn of the century in Paris, London, and Berlin rather than in America. And even though its first crusaders were American women, this new dance was seen as an international phenomenon, or a succession of them: first there was Loie Fuller in Paris (1892), with her veils and mysterious lights; then Isadora Duncan, starting around 1900 with free-form barefoot dancing in London, Paris, and Berlin; then after 1906, Ruth St. Denis in the same European capitals with her Oriental dance-dramas— and right on their heels, Diaghilev's Ballets Russes, which burst on the Paris scene in 1909 with a fabulous repertory that combined mysterious free-form and Oriental, composed by the young Michel Fokine—*Dance Polovetzian, Cléopatre, Le Carnaval, Schehérézade, Les Sylphides.* The Ballets Russes, unlike most of the solo dancers, kept growing and changing after World War I—by the twenties it had become Parisian, with its finger on the pulse of decorative arts and fashion. I will come back to the Ballets Russes in the twenties, because although it was dominated and guided by Diaghilev, a crucial chunk of its twenties repertory was created by a very intriguing woman choreographer, Bronislava Nijinska, the sister of Vaslav Nijinsky.

I want to turn now to America, where in the twenties our modern dance parted company with the Russian idea of modern dance. In

America this dance had begun as something unique, not as a revolution within an older dance form like Russia's classical ballet, but as a new solo mode, a personal expression, a kind of vision in the imagination of several young women. They were like Henry James's mythic American Girls, though they came from a poorer social class and they all got their start in some branch of the very lively popular American theater.

For present purposes we cannot go into the full stories of Loie Fuller, Isadora Duncan, and Ruth St. Denis, and point out the differences in their origins. Loie Fuller is the simplest to explain, a child actress and veteran of touring melodramas and extravaganzas, she became a dancer when she discovered that a beam of afternoon sun on her long skirt of china silk caused a fascinating effect, especially when she moved about. She perfected this effect and brought it to Paris—for Americans the mecca of art—and Paris in 1892 took her to be the highest flowering of the art nouveau imagination. Underneath the yards of whirling silk and the rainbow-hued lights, she was executing conventional vaudeville skirt-dance motions—but Fuller was a brilliant inventor of stage illusion, and she was elected to the French Academy of Sciences.

Loie Fuller's triumphant return to New York vaudeville in 1896 inspired younger dancer-ingénues in the New York theater, such as Isadora Duncan and Ruth St. Denis. These two came from similar backgrounds. Daughters of strong, embittered mothers, both were educated in feminist attitudes, militant health reform, and various aesthetic gymnastics (all these movements at that time were curiously of a piece). Ruth St. Denis's mother was a fanatic Methodist with a medical degree and a case of nervous prostration. Ruth went into vaudeville at age twelve to bring some income to the family; then she went to David Belasco's company, so it was not until age twenty-eight (1906) that she discovered, more or less unconsciously, a perfect metaphor for her feelings about art, theater, and religion—the Hindu legend of Radha the Holy Courtesan, which with full costumes and extras became her signature dance-drama.

Isadora Duncan is the key figure in this story—the one who changed dancing itself, who invented a new anatomical organization of the dancing body (not unrelated to advanced ideas in those years about clothes and gestures). My subject is not Duncan's flamboyant habits, her gallant but unruly life, but rather her art, which has been underrated. Patricia Meyer Spacks in *The Female Imagination* devotes a chapter to Duncan as the personification of women who fool themselves into thinking they're artists.[1] It seems she read Duncan's excessive, though witty, *My Life,* and forgot about her dancing.[2] But the dancing lives on in several women in New York who toured with Duncan's daughter-pupils in the twenties and thirties and who teach the Duncan dancing technique—which is quite straightforward—and the dances themselves, which have spatially clear and alive constructions and are not improvisations. Duncan's kind of dance reflected the cosmopolitan mix of San Francisco in her day: its rich theater life (the four Duncan children toured with their own variety show); the specialized musical awareness of Isadora's pianist mother; the social dancing, schottisches, mazurkas, quadrilles, which her sister taught to rich children; and the era's dress reform ideas about freeing women's bodies from tight lacing and layers of flannel undergarments about the waist. Duncan built her dance technique upon that maligned area—the solar plexus. This is where a Duncan dancer buoys herself up, at the lower ribs: preparing to move she draws in her ribs, then expands them to shoot forward or spring into the air. The chest, neck, and head follow.

I have dwelt on Isadora Duncan, whose career peaked before the twenties, because her story explains why this kind of interpretive dance began as a uniquely American and feminine phenomenon; and why it needed Europe to realize itself. America educated Duncan physically and theatrically, but Europe was where she, her siblings, and mother were compelled to go in order to satisfy that American hunger of those years—a bottomless craving for genuine art. When the theatrically experienced, imaginative, but undisciplined Duncan encountered Europe's paintings and sculptures, she acquired the discipline and the vision to record her wonderment through her own craft, dancing. Anyone who sees Duncan dances will recognize familiar poses of classical Greek Amazons, Dianas, and Venuses, plus gestures from Botticelli paintings, Matisse drawings, Rodin sculptures, Gordon Craig costume designs—all integrated into the spatial and musical mechanisms of the dances.

By the twenties, Duncan was a legend—a kind of giant influence-at-large. She had "mothered" many kinds of dance: besides American imitations she had partly inspired the Russian Michel Fokine in 1904 by her plastic expression and her unashamed raid on other art forms. In the twenties she gained new political significance by settling in the Soviet Union to teach the children of the new republic, and her dancing acquired new sculptural mass and intensity. In her final solos from her Soviet period she even experimented with stop-time techniques which resemble the Russian Sergei Eisenstein's bold modernistic films.

Let us go now to New York in the twenties and to Martha Graham, even though technically her mentor was not Isadora Duncan but Ruth St. Denis, through the California school of Denishawn (a combination of her name, Denis, and her husband's, [Ted] Shawn). Isadora remained in the background of dance, and in 1927, after her death, she loomed even larger as a ghost haunting all young dancers. Martha Graham was a new kind of person to be a dancer, not marginal, seedy gentility like Duncan and St. Denis, but a real middle-class girl, the oldest daughter of a doctor. She had no early dancing but went to college at the Cumnock School of Expression in Los Angeles, which taught that art and life are one and the same, and then on to Denishawn. After her father's death, her family fell on hard times. She went to work as a Denishawn vaudevillian, rose to a solo spot in a New York revue (the Greenwich Village Follies, a streamlined modern version of Ziegfeld), and in New York encountered the modern art theater which spurred her to find her own style of modern dance. Although she thus acquired some experience in the popular American theater, earlier in her art school education she had learned to respect the new European theater above all other varieties—as had most young Americans who became the theater intellectuals of the twenties. They did not go to live in Paris since they had to find ways to reach their audiences at home, but they were definitely European-inspired. Martha Graham, had she gone any-where, would not have chosen Paris, where Russian Ballet reigned supreme, but Germany where a militant and pure modern dance had emerged. However, she stayed home, traveled inside America, discov-ered the savage Indian-Hispanic culture of the Southwest, and made a vocabulary of New World actions: jumps repeated over and over, back-ward falls in perfect control, taut rolls on the ground, stiff strides, and, of course, the famous mobilization of the torso called "contract, release"—an intensification of Duncan's breathing through the solar plexus. Martha Graham was Duncan's child in the sense that she made up her actions out of her own body: center stage was the center of her body and the architecture of her dances was a construction from the inside out. But she grew up to convert Duncan's lyricism into a sup-pressed, staccato modern song to match the modern city and the geome-try of everything around her. She codified dance. In leaving her I want to register a note of mourning for her dismissal of the great musical comedy jazz dancers of the twenties: Fred and Adele Astaire, Marilyn Miller, Ann Pennington, Gilda Gray—who commanded a genre which, though eclectic, was highly evolved, witty, and craftsmanlike. Martha Graham and the other art dancers ignored this as material for their work, except in muted, distant reflections.

I will end with Paris. Martha Graham in New York was a great and grave theatrical genius, but in her search for pure art she excluded a whole realm of loose, witty, rhythmic dancing. In Paris, Bronia Nijinska had become the opposite sort of creator, absorbing ideas into her idiom instead of shutting them out. In 1921 Nijinska staged *Sleeping Beauty* for Diaghilev, showing her mastery of the classical dance-and-mime tradition—and went on in the early twenties to redefine classicism in such varied works as *Les Noces,* a stark, vigorous stylization of Russian peasant rites set to Stravinsky music, and *Les Biches,* a perfumed satire of a twenties party with an outré hostess—a haughty garçonne in blue velvet tunic—some girls in pink feathers, and three beautiful boys, all dancing to a Poulenc score. In these works the ambiguous romantic essence of classical ballet was reexperienced. Nijinska's fascination for us today arises not from her androgynous appearance which was very like that of her famous brother Vaslav—she was short, almost squat, with Mongol eyes and an inevitable cigarette in a long, thin holder—but from her objective, androgynous mind. Nijinska focused and incorporated new ideas, steps, and behavior into the classical tradition, while she reassembled the past for the newly expatriated Russian Ballet and bequeathed it to them. She passed the torch of neoclassicism to Diaghilev's youngest choreographer, George Balanchine, who is still holding it high at our own New York City Ballet.

NOTES

1. Patricia Meyer Spacks, *The Female Imagination* (New York: Knopf, 1975).
2. Isadora Duncan, *My Life* (New York: Boni & Liveright, 1927).

13.

Women's Voices

Ned Rorem

Let me make four statements, each a variation on the theme at hand, and each a theme in itself to be varied in due course.

1. French emphasis on music was weaker than on the other arts of the 1920s for two reasons. First, France has never been a musical country. It has produced great composers and performers, but the French public, expert at looking, tasting, and dressing, is intractable where listening is concerned. Second, rhythms of evolution in the various arts do not synchronize, and music usually drags behind the rest. The centuries are sprinkled with names of women in politics, literature, painting, and science. But music, although probably the oldest art, is nevertheless the youngest, being the last to flower as personal expression: the composer as individual is a very recent development. Thus the 1920s can claim no musical equivalent of a Djuna Barnes as American in Paris, or of an Elinor Wylie as American in New York.

There was, however, a Parisian in Paris, eventually to become a Parisian in America. So far as musical pedagogy is concerned—and by extension musical creation—she is the most influential person who ever lived. Nadia Boulanger came from a highly musical family, and won a Prix de Rome at twenty. Her younger sister Lili, also a composer, was more creatively gifted, according to Nadia who was the girl's only mentor. When Lili died in 1918, the grief-stricken Nadia forsook all thought of her own composition, and devoted the rest of her life to promoting Lili's posthumous work by helping other composers to realize themselves. Before 1920, American musicians always went to Germany for their postgraduate grand tour. When the young Aaron Copland, in 1921, wandered into Boulanger's harmony class at Fountainebleau and was overwhelmed at the woman's ability to bring her dull subject to life, he opened a trend toward France which continued for half a century. Every composer during that period was touched, at least indirectly, by Nadia Boulanger; American music gained its identity through her indelible aegis. Because women have traditionally not been teachers of composition, Boulanger's listing in the Conservatoire catalog was always "Professor of Accompaniment."

2. Throughout the world, musical creative pulse is at present less stimulated than that of movies or books. But it does throb along and perhaps most healthily in the United States. If I had to name the six best living American composers, three of them would be Barbara Kolb, Lucia Dlugoszewski, and Louise Talma. The sole realm of productivity that cannot be accurately located, generalized, or defined is the artist's. The sole human endeavor that cannot be replicated—unlike making bread, money, wise remarks, or babies—is the work of art. No sooner do we define the true artist's behavior than another true artist misbehaves. No sooner do we conveniently frame one art work than a second overflows its borders. We cannot therefore speak of women composers but of each woman as she appears, since each one, through her work which is final and unique, provides her own definition.

3. Being a composer, I naturally stress the creative aspect of my art—although music, like theater and dance (but unlike painting and poetry), divides neatly into making and doing, which are often remote from each other. Women as performers have done well over the past few hundred years. In France, during the teens of this century, women come preeminently to mind as interpreters of Debussy and Ravel: singers Mary Garden, Jeanne Bathori, and Madeleine Grey; pianist Marguerite Long and violinist Helene Jourdan-Morhange. Even as patrons, women seemed more in evidence than men: Misia Sert, for instance, or the Princesse de Polignac, Ida Rubinstein, who commissioned what turned out to be many a musical masterpiece; or even the Bostonian Mrs. Richard J. Hall, who premiered Debussy's saxophone *Rapsodie* back in 1895. But these people had vanished by 1919, and a new crop did not sprout until the thirties. The twenties were not rich in performers of either sex. As for women composers, France produced only two in the

twenties: Marcelle de Manziarly and Germaine Tailleferre, both first-rate and thriving today; and America, only one: the late Ruth Crawford, a real innovator, but her sounds turned more pedestrian with the political overlay of the next decade. (Crawford, incidentally, was the mother of folk singer Pete Seeger.) How have women composers been treated? All composers of all sexes are less discriminated against than merely ignored, for they are expendable. Performing musicians are an investment, and since female singers, like actresses (as opposed to female painters, like cellists), are needed, they can demand and get equal pay.

4. Why have there been so few women composers? English critic Cecil Gray once gallantly explained that music—the very muse of music—being feminine, needed a man to manipulate her. "All artists," said Picasso, "are half man and half woman, and the woman is insufferable." If we all contain within us man, woman, and child, how then to distinguish between men, women, and children? If the obvious reply is that all contain all, but not in equal parts, the next question becomes: What is the difference in kind between the womanly part of a woman and the womanly part of a man? An art work could be defined as the result of a marriage of the true minds; the minds are within one individual. Could a case be made that even the greatest women have never given way to the same vast flights of fancy as men? Even the grand failure seems a male prerogative, except maybe for Gertrude Stein. Is it conceivable that a work of art is the result of the effort of a single person to produce offspring—the self-pollinating hermaphrodite giving birth?

In 1970, my friend Robin Morgan turned on me with the words: "Stick to men poets. Sylvia Plath belongs to our sisters." As though poetry belonged to anyone, even the poet, once it is written! Still, maybe Robin had a point. If I feel no more need for Plath, it is precisely because she *was* a woman and I am not, not even metaphorically. Not that a composer need feel, or even respect, a poem in order to set it well. And masterpieces that thrill are more impossible to musicalize than lesser verses that ring a bell. The question of which composers select which poets to set to music, and how they set the poems selected, is engrossing. A woman's setting of Plath poems might not be better than mine, but it will be different, not only because the woman composer is another person, but because she is female. How to prove the difference? Is there more difference between a man and a woman than between one good composer and another?

Mendelssohn's sister Fanny composed. Mendelssohn advised her against turning professional but did include anonymously some of her songs in a published collection of his own pieces. Queen Victoria sang, and once programmed a song from the Mendelssohn collection. When the composer discovered that the song was Fanny's, he felt duty-bound to admit this to his sister and the queen. Collections are mischievous when it comes to art, which is why art never flourishes at the start of a revolution; art is not community but the lonely voice. There is no women's art, but only art by a woman. Is it not possible that what one sometimes senses as the mediocrity pervasive in all expression since World War II stems from our emphasis on *who* produces rather than on *what* is produced—the *who* being collections instead of single souls?

PART IV

Attitudes toward Creative Women

Introduction

The perspectives, accomplishments, and culture of women have until recently been neglected in histories. In the 1970s, a scholarly revolution in the field of history emerged to challenge the old assumptions by many that the world of men deserved exclusive attention; women have now become the subject of much research. Although present interest in women's history began with a simple desire to recover a lost heritage, it soon moved beyond this goal. The new women's history seeks to consider realms of human experience—through varied research methodologies and unique source materials—that had heretofore been left unexplored.

Blanche Wiesen Cook argues that conscious feminism and politics have been diminished if not erased from the twenties. What books are available, often written by male authors, indicate that women never showed concern with politics. Instead, she says, where women worked with men, their activities, as with the rest of feminine history, slipped into obscurity. As examples of her thesis, Cook examines the political statements and actions of two women, Natalie Barney and Crystal Eastman. Only through a reassessment of these women's lives and those of others from the twenties, Cook states, can we know about their political contributions.

William O'Neill, in examining the changing times of the 1920s, points out several important influences on women. People no longer felt that women differed from men so radically as to be incapable of doing anything outside the home. Moving into the workplace, they began to accept positions in untraditional fields. Changes also occurred in standards of personal conduct and morality—women became freer. In the short run, these changes manifested themselves in the flapper image, and over time, in the sexual revolution that continues. Free at last, women artists began to work out of their inner, rather than social selves. The result was an outpouring of artistic energy.

O'Neill, in comparing feminists of the 1920s and today, states that both believed a better woman makes for a better world. The old feminism, however, emphasized that a woman better equipped to help others was also better able to help herself. The new feminism puts self-interest above general reforms. Whatever approach is taken, he says, we all profit from the free expression of great talents.

14.

Women and Politics: The Obscured Dimension

Blanche Wiesen Cook

When we think about women in the 1920s in Paris and New York a variety of images comes easily to mind. Images of flappers, bobbed hair, and cigarette holders; women in intimate conversations sipping Pernod on the terrace of the Select; women selling and promoting the books of great men in their bookstores; and more recently, women dancing together in bars and salons. We might be jolted by images of women at the speaker's podium delivering electrifying feminist speeches, many of which assailed militarism and proclaimed revolution.

The exclusion of such images, historically as real as the others, has resulted in the trivialization of women's role in society. Political women acting on behalf of their own needs, visions, and work—not acting out of the prescribed role of wife or benefactress—have until recently been permitted to disappear from our collective memory. The disappearance of women from political life has worked to obscure the existence of a cohesive women's culture that was at once profoundly feminist and political. One result of the disappearance of women from political life and feminism from history is the almost inevitable subordination of women artists in popular culture. Women artists, writers, poets are defined as eccentrics and salonists who served history by discovering and nurturing great male talents. Where a great female talent is too undeniable even for the popular culture, a new category for women was created: the genius manqué.

Not only have women's creative contributions been devalued, the very meaning of their lives has been distorted as it filtered through the patriarchal sensibilities of our culture. The current vogue regarding Paris in the 1920s, for example, seems to feature books about lesbians too often written out of that sensibility. We read about lesbian flirtations, details of gifts they exchanged, and their varied costumes. We read nothing about feminist consciousness among lesbians. This is not because lesbians were not feminists, but because men and male-identified women continue to write their histories.

Insofar as we read about lesbians in the popular culture—whether it is about Romaine Brooks, Adrienne Monnier, or Natalie Clifford Barney— we read about their service to men, their sacrifice toward publication and celebration of men's work, their maternal nurturing of sensitive, artistic male talents, and, of course, their love affairs with men—no matter how isolated, transient, or uninteresting they may have been. We may read about their relations with each other too—but rarely in terms of their own work, their own enthusiasms, and almost never in terms of the support, energy, and strength they derived from each other's company, from the affection and love they shared. The fact that they created a community of commitment where on a regular basis they read, worked over, and improved each other's writings is largely ignored.

For years the very existence of women like Natalie Barney was left out of history books. Ironically, the two recent books on her life are by men [1] (several women are seriously studying her life and work). It is interesting to compare George Wickes's 1976 work on Natalie Barney with one of the only references about her written previously. In 1947 Sam Putnam wrote that Natalie Barney ran the only "real salon . . . possibly in all the world." And from her salon Barney exerted extraordinary power. She "made" Paul Valéry, for example. And when she was miffed, her temporary disfavor, wrote Putnam, had the power to "unmake" him. Woman as goddess; woman as witch. The stereotypes in this book abound. To her salon, Sam Putnam tells us, "Proust used to come . . . and Gide, and others." He lists them all, not one woman by name: "France's leading men of letters, academicians, members of the Institute, Sorbonne professors, beautiful ladies, even a stray countess or two." [2]

George Wickes tells us a lot more than that—not the least important of which is that most of Natalie Barney's salons were for women only. He tells us that Barney was a legend in her own time, the most notorious seductress of the most desirable women in Paris. He tells us the women "gossipped." He tells us of the tribulations of their frequent flirtations and occasional affairs. He tells us that Barney was cynical about love and he separates love from the lifelong friendships she worked vigorously to sustain. Wickes treats friendship among women with very little insight. And for him, lesbianism appears to be limited to fleeting moments of lust amidst hours of longing.

I do not mean to be unfair to George Wickes and I am grateful for the information he provides. He, like all of us, is a product of our culture and time. It is dangerous to analyze people's motives; I do not know why Wickes wrote this particular book on Barney. But there is an element of male voyeurism in the treatment of the lives of these women that has nothing to do with why women are searching the past. We are searching the past not only because Gertrude Stein told us to look for the questions, but because the past has some useful models that might alter and enhance our own vision and options as we move from the male dominance of patriarchy to more equalitarian relations and choices—to a fully creative and unconfined society.

In a recent article on female support networks and their essential value in the lives of public and active women, I referred to the prejudices of our culture that have rendered it more acceptable to label perfectly ordinary and highly regarded women as asexual spinsters rather than lesbians. In other work I have explored the deradicalization of our political history so that the very existence of radical movements has been truncated, minimized; and where radical theory has existed among respectable men and women it has been diminished, falsified into reformism, and otherwise belittled when not entirely erased.[3] Until recently when we sought information about women in Paris and New York in the 1920s we discovered several poets, fewer painters, Janet Flanner who gave us Paris, Sylvia Beach who gave us her almost frank memoirs, and Djuna Barnes. In addition we discovered some "illicit" behavior, a lot of horseback riding, and some high fashion. But no conscious feminism and no politics.

We must begin with basics. Women's personal relationship to power is very basic; it is a profoundly political relationship. Women-identified women, who neither seek male protection nor court male approval, make a very specific statement about the power of patriarchy. Very simply, in their own lives, they reject it. And that is a very political act. We must begin to examine the implications of their lives and the full dimensions of their work.

We have only just begun to learn the rudimentary facts of their lives. We do not know their attitude toward the organized feminist movement. We do not know whether they attended the international feminist meeting that brought thousands of women to Paris in May 1926. And if they scorned the public feminist activity that swirled around them, appearing daily in the press, we need to know out of what class or political consciousness they removed themselves from the issues that concerned so many of their contemporaries. But we have no reason to believe they excluded themselves—except for the omission of any reference to those activities by our dominant culture. Wickes tells us, for example, that Natalie Barney in 1968 was oblivious to the politics that halted all Paris. And, he asserts, "she was never one to pay attention to what was happening in the streets." But Natalie Barney organized pacifist meetings in 1917—and that was a very courageous and extraordinary thing to do. Then, feminist politics were not happening in the streets. And when fascist politics were happening in the streets Barney and her friends were remarkably ambivalent. Wickes's contempt for political activity may or may not reflect Barney's—his book gives us little opportunity to find out. He devoted only two paragraphs to her early pacifism and her later reactionary political views.

We are only beginning to do this kind of research. My own research—ten years of work on New York women associated with the 1920s—only recently enabled me to rescue from total obscurity one of the most dashing and crusading political figures in the United States. Crystal Eastman was a feminist and a socialist. A tough labor lawyer, she was one of the principal investigators of the celebrated Pittsburgh survey. Out of that experience she wrote *Work Accidents and the Law*, and in 1910, as the first woman commissioner appointed to office in New York State, drafted the first Workers' Compensation Act, which became the model law used throughout the United States. During World War I she founded the Women's Peace Party of New York and encouraged Jane Addams to create a national party, now called the Women's International League for Peace and Freedom. As executive director of the American Union against Militarism, she and her assistant Roger Baldwin organized the Civil Liberties Bureau, renamed the American Civil Liberties Union. She was identified with the militant wing of the British and United States equal rights movement, and was one of the four original founders of Alice Paul's Congressional Union which introduced the ERA in 1923. After the war she and her brother Max Eastman coedited *The Liberator*. Her dedication to the success of the Russian Revolution which the women's peace journal she headed, *Four Lights*, hailed with "mad, glad joy," resulted in her being tailed by FBI agents and informers. Their notes provide an extensive FBI file useful for historical reclamation.

How could such a woman get lost from history? It was easy. Where she worked with men, her male associates, Roger Baldwin and Max Eastman, for example, were credited for her work. Where she worked with women, their activities with all the rest of our feminist history slipped into obscurity. For fifty years our entire culture militated so vigorously against our discovering Crystal Eastman's ideas and finding them usable that she temporarily disappeared from history. After her early death in 1928 there were memorials and obituaries. But from that year to this not one essay, not one book has been entirely devoted to her work or to her life. The only historian who has attempted to write about her in detail said mistakenly that Crystal Eastman "had no audience for her views; the unpublished nature of her writing attests to the fact that the publishers did not consider her concerns worthy of print."[4]

Almost everything Crystal Eastman wrote was published. She had an enthusiastic and dedicated audience in the United States and England. She wrote for newspapers as well as magazines. She wrote boldly and well. She was paid for what she wrote, sufficiently to live for several years largely on that income. A chance remark by her friend Jeannette Lowe encouraged me to look for her writings. Lowe said simply that Crystal wrote feminist articles for money. It enabled her to travel; she wrote for a living. Her articles enabled them to summer in the South of France with their children and usually without their husbands.[5]

Crystal Eastman's ideas were heretical and dangerous. Jeannette Lowe said that she was incredibly free. Her life embodied a threat to customary order. How was history to appraise the militant feminist wing of the international "smart set"? How could history appraise the life of a woman who was not only a mother but also a socialist? Until recently by denying her existence altogether.

In May 1926 in Paris, Crystal Eastman, who believed that "women's interests today are as wide as the world," proclaimed that "the future is with us." There is no doubt about that. But the future demands a thorough reexamination of the past. It is not enough to know about the women of Paris and New York through a selective filter. We want to know the details of their lives, their thoughts, and how they survived in a world in which women are not expected to survive except in terms of men and in service to men. To recreate the past in a thorough fashion is no idle fantasy. It has taken long for the dead weight of Leonard Woolf to be removed so that the full range of Virginia Woolf's work might emerge. Recent studies raise deeper and more connective questions. Did Bloomsbury ever connect with Paris—with New York? Did Paris ever connect with New York—with Bloomsbury? How were the connections made? What were they for? Crystal Eastman's daughter has pictures of Crystal with Leonard Woolf outside the Woolfs' home. They are intimate smiling pictures. Yet there is no written evidence that they ever knew one another. A chance photograph, a chance memory gives us so much to look for. We have only just begun.

NOTES

1. George Wickes, *The Amazon of Letters: The Life and Loves of Natalie Barney* (New York: G.P. Putnam's Sons, 1976). Also Jean Chalon, *Portrait d' une séductrice* (Paris: Stock, 1976).
2. Sam Putnam, *Paris Was Our Mistress* (New York: Viking, 1947), pp. 73-74.
3. Blanche Wiesen Cook, "Female Support Networks and Political Activism: Lillian Wald, Crystal Eastman, Emma Goldman," *Chrysalis* no. 3, (1977): pp. 43-66.
4. June Sochen, *Movers and Shakers* (New York: Quadrangle, 1973), pp. 48-49.
5. Crystal Eastman, "Marriage under Two Roofs." In *Crystal Eastman on Women and Revolution,* ed. Blanche Wiesen Cook (New York: Oxford University Press, 1978), pp. 76-85.

15.

Reflections on Feminism: Implications for Today

William L. O'Neill

This volume is a tribute to the generation of women artists of the 1920s. It is a celebration in their honor as well as an effort to understand them and their time and the places where they worked. The basis of the contributions was the delight and inspiration generated by our subjects, and the gratitude we felt for them in consequence. There was a touch of wonder too, as always must be felt when confronting greatly talented people. In the end, art comes from the interaction of creator and medium, a mysterious process never fully understood, even by the artist.

But there is a scholarship of art even so that seeks to explain when and why things happen. As we are mostly scholars and critics, our efforts were often directed to that end. Many chapters concern themselves with the origins of one or another art or artist. But the key observation, applying in some degree to all, was made by Sara Via Pais. She points out, in connection with a poem by Louise Bogan, that the artist works out of the deep self, which women have always been taught to repress in favor of the social self. In the twenties for the first time an atmosphere had emerged that enabled women to assert themselves as never before. They could now claim, as men always had, the right to use everything—to explore their deep selves. The result was that outpouring of artistic energy we have been discussing.

There was irony in this, for most of our artists were not themselves active feminists in the organizational sense, nor were they exactly what suffragists had in mind when campaigning for equal rights. The older feminists had believed that when women gained legal equality social reforms would multiply. They had not supposed that women would necessarily run for office in large numbers. They did expect that women would vote together in favor of candidates who stood for peace, family welfare, public health, and other traditional womanly concerns. As we know, this failed to happen. Women did not vote as a bloc and, especially at first, a great many did not vote at all. Political life was not transformed or even elevated as had been prophesied.

Several other things did take place—not because women gained the vote, but on account of the preceding years of agitation and education. In the nineteenth century most people appear to have thought that women differed from men so radically as to be incapable of doing anything outside the home well or safely. The effect of feminism, first rhetorically and then by example, was to undermine this belief. Women entered the professions, took up sport, and broadened their sphere of action enormously. Accordingly, the vote did not confer equality upon women so much as it recognized what they had already achieved. Much remained to be done—and still does—before women would enjoy the same benefits as men. But to an extent Victorians thought was impossible, women had earned the right to function independently.

There were two large areas in which this liberation had the greatest effect. One concerned personal behavior and morality. In the nineteenth century, feminists and moral reformers had struggled to destroy the double standard of morality according to which women were expected to be virtuous and men sinful. Their idea had been to achieve a single standard of rectitude for both sexes. In this they failed, not only because vice proved to be more difficult to abolish than they thought, but even more because women, once given the chance, saw the problem differently. What they wanted, it became clear in the 1920s, was not so much to restrict men as to be freer themselves. This meant in the short run the flapper, and over time the sexual revolution that is still going on. There is indeed a single standard of morals, in sight if not in hand, but opposite to what had been expected.

The other great change, and from the standpoint of older feminists a less unwelcome one, was the further movement of women into untraditional fields. There would be female aviators, professional athletes, and female artists—not for the first time but in greater numbers and working in more varied ways than anyone would have guessed. Free at last to mine their deepest selves, women artists lavished gifts upon a startled world.

Inevitably one asks what this means today, when a new generation of feminists has taken up the work abandoned several generations ago. Clearly it does not mean that a feminist art can materialize on demand. The women artists of the twenties did not deal with specifically feminist themes. And they did not come forth because instructed to do so. Nor did they have a sense of themselves as part of a common enterprise, save to the degree that they, along with male colleagues, were swept along by the great current of modernism rushing through the arts. Only in retrospect can we see that the women artists of the period had been lifted up together by the rising tide of feminine self-confidence.

The feminism of today does not guarantee there will be a new wave of women artists tomorrow. Nor should such a possibility be ruled out. We have been assuming that women flourished as artists because feminism allowed them to be as ruthlessly self-centered as great artists traditionally have been but women were always conditioned not to be. This message is even stronger now than it was when women took their first big steps toward freedom. The old feminism, though arising from wounded feelings of women who had been unjustly treated, emphasized the social side. Women should be free so as to benefit society, was the favored argument. It turned out that the woman who was better equipped to help others was also better able to help herself.

Feminists today are more self-aware. They too believe that a better woman makes for a better world. But they are readier to put their own interests first, leaving more general reforms for a later date. One sees this most clearly in lesbian feminists, and in the vast literature presenting divorce as an instrument of growth. Such changes are not always wanted, especially by men. And some radicals wonder whether women really need to be liberated as much as other groups. If putting one's self first is what artists must be able to do, then women must have the same license as men if they are to be as creative.

In the end, the artist's selfishness or self-centeredness serves a larger purpose. These 1920s women did not work with the idea of benefiting humanity or even their own sex. We all profited just the same, as society always does from the free expression of great talents. This is the lesson to be drawn from the present effort, one that I hope will be underscored by the new women's movement going on today.

About the Editors and Contributors

Helen Krich Chinoy is professor of theater at Smith College. Among her publications are *Actors on Acting* and *Directors on Directing*, both edited with Tony Cole; *Reunion: A Self-Portrait of the Group Theatre;* and her latest work, *Women in the American Theatre*, coauthored with Linda W. Jenkins. She is associate editor of *Theatre Journal* and serves on the Research Commission of the American Theatre Association, of which she was made a fellow in 1980. Also, she is chair of the Research Commission of the American Society for Theatre Research.

Blanche Wiesen Cook is professor of history at John Jay College of Criminal Justice, City University of New York. She is known principally for her work on political and peace movements. She is senior editor of the Garland Library Series on War and Peace and the author of *Crystal Eastman on Women and Revolution* and *The Declassified Eisenhower: A Divided Legacy.* A syndicated columnist and member of the editorial board of *Peace and Change,* she has written several articles on women and political activism in the 1920s.

Robert D. Cottrell is professor of Romance languages at Ohio State University and an expert on French literature. He has written many articles and book reviews, his interest centering on the sixteenth and twentieth centuries. Among his books on authors from the latter periods are *Brantôme: The Writer as Portraitist of His Age; Alain on Happiness;*

Colette; Simone De Beauvoir; and his recent work *Sexuality/Texuality: A Study of the Fabric of Montaigne's Essays.* His current research is a study of Marguerite de Navarre's poetry.

Ann Douglas is associate professor of English at Columbia University, where she teaches American literature and culture. She is widely published in the fields of American studies and women's studies; her most recent book, *The Feminization of American Culture,* combines both interests. She is a member of the editorial board of *Women's Studies* and coeditor of the *American Men and Women of Letters Series.*

Hugh D. Ford, well known for his articles and books on American authors and publishers of the 1920s who resided in Paris, is professor of English at Trenton State College. Among his books on this period are *Nancy Cunard: Brave Poet; The Left Bank Revisited; Published in Paris;* and a forthcoming work, *Paris Portraits: Six Americans in Paris.* The recipient of numerous prestigious fellowships, his latest research concerns the letters of Nancy Cunard.

Emily Hahn, a well-known author and lecturer, is a prolific writer, having published a book a year for the last fifty years of her professional career. These works include biographies, reportage, memoirs, and fiction. Her latest books are *Look Who's Talking!* and *Love of Gold.* On the staff of *The New Yorker,* her prior positions have included mining engineer, newspaperwoman, and college instructor.

Carolyn G. Heilbrun, a well-known author and lecturer, is professor of English at Columbia University. She has written numerous articles, many of which concern women and women's issues, and books such as *Lady Ottoline's Album; Toward a Recognition of Androgyny;* and *Reinventing Womanhood.* She serves on the editorial boards of *Twentieth Century Literature* and *Signs.* She is a frequent contributor to the weekly *New York Times* series "Hers."

Anne Hollander, an art critic and an art and dress historian, has written extensively for many journals, including the *New Republic* and *New York Magazine.* Her recently published book, *Seeing Through Clothes,* examines the relationship of fashion to art. Currently she is at work on two other publications, one involving dress in the movies and the other a history of illustration. In addition to her research and writing, she is a costume designer for stage and television productions.

Maureen Howard, currently a visiting professor of English at Amherst College, has taught and lectured at many American institutions of higher education. A free-lance writer, she has published numerous novels, stories, criticism, and other works. Among her publications are an autobiography, *Facts of Life,* an edited anthology, *Seven American Women Writers of the Twentieth Century,* and the novels *Not a Word about Nightingales; Bridgeport Bus;* and *Before My Time.* She has been both a Guggenheim and a Radcliffe Institute fellow.

Elizabeth Kendall, a free-lance dance critic, is currently a fellow of the New York Institute for the Humanities at New York University. The author of *Where She Danced: American Dancing, 1880-1930,* she is currently writing a book on Hollywood romantic film comedies in the 1930s. She is the author of two television scripts—"Trailblazers of Modern Dance" and "Pilobolus"—that were part of the WNET dance series. The recipient of a Rockefeller grant in 1975, she has studied the Duncan technique as well as ballet and modern dance.

Virginia Lee Lussier, assistant provost at Rutgers University, New Brunswick campus, is coeditor of *Women, the Arts, and the 1920s in Paris and New York.* As a political scientist, she has written a variety of articles on Latin America, conflict resolution, and academic collective bargaining, which have appeared in *The Journal of Conflict Resolution, The Journal of Higher Education,* and the *Labor Law Journal,* among others. She has written several articles on women and is coeditor of *Women's Lives: Perspectives on Progress and Change.*

William L. O'Neill is professor of history at Rutgers University. He has published many books on twentieth-century American social and political history and on American women. Among his works in the latter area are *Everyone Was Brave: The Rise and Fall of Feminism in America* and three edited volumes, *The Women's Movement: Feminism in the United States and England; The American Sexual Dilemma;* and *Women at Work.* His latest book is *The Last Romantic: The Life of Max Eastman.*

Sara Via Pais, educated in French studies and comparative cultural history, is presently manager of Affiliated Communications at Home Box Office, a cable television network. Author of *Paul Alexis et Emile Zola: l'héritage du naturalisme,* she has another book in progress, *Venice in the European Literary Imagination, 1850-1914.* A Fulbright fellow in 1968, she has been an assistant professor at both the University of Lille and Princeton University.

Ned Rorem, a noted composer and author, has been the recipient of numerous prestigious fellowships, awards, and prizes, including two

Pulitzers for his work in musical composition. Among his works are symphonies, choral arrangements, and compositions for individual instruments. As an author, he has written many magazine articles and books, such as *The Paris Diary of Ned Rorem; The New York Diary; Music and People;* and his latest work, *An Absolute Gift.*

Cynthia Secor is director of HERS Mid Atlantic (Higher Education Resources Services) located at the University of Pennsylvania. She has written articles on women and administration that have appeared in *Change* magazine and *The Annals,* among others, and on twentieth-century novelists, principally Gertrude Stein, that have appeared in journals such as *Women's Studies* and *Contemporary Novelist.* She has two forthcoming books, one on Gertrude Stein and another on careers for women in higher education.

Catharine R. Stimpson, professor of English at Rutgers University, has published widely in literature and women's studies. For six years, until 1980, she served as editor of the foremost journal in the field, *Signs: Journal of Women in Culture and Society.* She is a member of the editorial board of *Women's Studies: An Interdisciplinary Journal* and *Critical Inquiry,* and is active in various national committees devoted to women's concerns. Her most recent publications are a novel, *Class Notes,* and an edited volume with Ethel S. Person entitled *Women, Sex, and Sexuality.*

Cheryl A. Wall is assistant professor of English at Rutgers University. She has written articles on the Harlem Renaissance, such as "Paris and Harlem: Two Culture Capitals" and on Black women writers, such as Zora Neale Hurston, Gwendolyn Brooks, and Frances Watkins Harper. A Fulbright scholar, she is presently completing her first book, *Women of the Harlem Renaissance.* She serves as a member of the Committee of Consultants for *American Women Writers,* a three volume reference work.

Kenneth W. Wheeler is provost of Rutgers University, New Brunswick campus, and university professor of history. An urban historian, he has published *To Wear a City's Crown,* an edited volume, *For the Union,* and is coeditor of *Women, the Arts, and the 1920s in Paris and New York.* His current research concerns nineteenth-century municipal services in Boston, Paris, and New York.